Fancy's Craft

Fancy's Craft

*Art and Identity in the Early Works
of Djuna Barnes*

Cheryl J. Plumb

*Selinsgrove: Susquehanna University Press
London and Toronto: Associated University Presses*

Associated University Presses
440 Forsgate Drive
Cranbury, NJ   08512

Associated University Presses
25 Sicilian Avenue
London WC1A 2QH, England

Associated University Presses
2133 Royal Windsor Drive
Unit 1
Mississauga, Ontario
Canada   L5J 1K5

. The paper used in this publication meets the requirements of the American National Standard for Permanence of Paper for Printed Library Materials Z39.48-1984.

Library of Congress Cataloging-in-Publication Data

Plumb, Cheryl J., 1943–
  Fancy's craft.

  Bibliography: p.
  Includes index.
  1. Barnes, Djuna—Criticism and interpretation.
I. Title.
PS3503.A614Z84   1986   818'.5209   85-62679
ISBN 0-941664-17-1 (alk. paper)

Printed in the United States of America

My love and thanks to my parents, Keith and Bernice, and to my son, Hylon, who, while I wrote, grew up to become "captain of himself."

Contents

Acknowledgments

For their thoughtful reading, advice, and encouragement, I am indebted to Professors Robert D. Hume and Wendell V. Harris. My thanks go also to the librarians and staff of the University of Maryland Special Collections.

In addition, I am grateful to the Penn State/York Campus Advisory Board and to the Commonwealth Education System for financial support to assist me in the completion of this book.

Finally, a word of thanks to all of the colleagues and friends who have listened and encouraged; they are too numerous to mention but too important to forget.

I am grateful to the following publishers, who have graciously granted me permission to use copyrighted material: to St. Martin's Press, Inc., New York, for material from *Ryder*; to the Authors League Fund, New York, for material from *Ladies Almanack, To the Dogs, Three from the Earth,* and *The Dove*; to Faber and Faber, London, for material from *Spillway and Other Stories*. Excerpts from "A Night among the Horses," "The Passion," "The Rabbit," The Valet," "Aller et Retour," "Spillway," "Cassation," "The Grande Malade" from *The Selected Works of Djuna Barnes*. Copyright 1923 by Boni & Liveright, Inc. Copyright renewed 1950 by Djuna Barnes. Copyright © 1962 by Djuna Barnes. Reprinted by permission of the Estate of Djuna Barnes and Farrar, Straus and Giroux, Inc. My request to quote material from Djuna Barnes's letters has been granted by permission Special Collections, University of Maryland Libraries, College Park.

9

Fancy's Craft

Introduction

As an expatriate of the twenties and thirties, Djuna Barnes has been categorized as an obscure and private writer. While she has received the attention of a small number of critics, her fiction has remained outside the American literary mainstream. This may be attributed to the difficulty of her prose and perhaps also to her subject matter: early plays and poems treated sexuality, specifically woman's sexuality, with a frankness that created a temporary literary sensation but little sustained interest. Another factor may be that Barnes's early prose appeared while the American literary tradition was dominated by realism and naturalism represented by Stephen Crane, Theodore Dreiser, Frank Norris, Sinclair Lewis, and Sherwood Anderson. These writers were recognized as experimental, particularly with respect to subject matter.

More daring in subject matter and verbal experiment, Barnes's early work does not fit comfortably with the features of realism and naturalism. While experimental in subject matter and psychological motivation, Barnes approaches character and plot differently. Her characters are often types; she combines abstract suggestion with psychological intensity. Significantly, except for those of the earliest newspaper tales, her plots depend less on chronological, causal development than upon thematic juxtaposition. In manner she is less sentimental than Anderson and Dreiser and more ironic in her handling of character. Her tone and vision anticipate black humorists of recent years.[1] In general, Barnes's experimentation has more in common with writers who moved beyond realist and naturalist traditions, writers like her contemporaries Eugene O'Neill in drama and T. S. Eliot and Ezra Pound in poetry—heirs of the symbolist tradition who have been readily accepted into the mainstream of American literature.

Let us consider briefly, then, the symbolist context before we examine those assumptions and methods in Barnes's early journalism, one-acts, short fiction, and in the two works that round out her early career, *Ryder* and *Ladies Almanack*. Once Barnes's work is set against a background of symbolist assumptions and methods, it becomes clear that her work consistently focuses on consciousness and moral integrity and on the superior sensibility, represented in her work by artist figures. Throughout her early work she criticizes social values that narrowly define the individual sensibility. Within this context her art, rich in its complexity, is discovered to be centrally related to a dialogue that had dominated American literature, a dialogue between individual values and identity and social conformity.

In its historical context symbolism was not only a technique, a way of communicating indirectly, but also a complex of themes and ideas about reality and the perception of reality that formed in opposition to the theory and practice of naturalism. J.-K. Huysmans (in *A Rebours*, originally published in 1884) and Rémy de Gourmont (in the preface to *Le Livres des Masques*, 1896) pointed out the limitations of naturalism and adopted concepts to move beyond its conventions. Huysmans felt naturalism had done its work, "the service of showing real personages in accurate surroundings," and he objected to it because it was bound by "the delineation of everyday existence." Like Gourmont, Huysmans asserted the need to abandon "traditional plots of intrigue."[2] Each emphasized idea, rather than an individual life, as the organizing principle of a work. Gourmont applauded the tendency of symbolism "to take from life only the characteristic detail, to pay attention only to the act by which a man distinguishes himself from other men, to realize only results—essences."[3]

These ideas have interesting consequences. Fiction that exploits idea as an organizing principle is likely to disregard chronological development of plot and characters. But since character serves idea, readers can expect that characters may be given as types rather than fully developed. Similarly, illustrative scenes or moments of revelation replace traditional plot. Instead of chronological progression, the approved method of organization exploits thematic repetition, that is, musical structure. The reader is to associate themes and symbols presented without the aid of direct authorial comment. Thus, themes or ideas are presented indirectly. In addition, fiction that focuses on "characteristic detail," or the "act by which a man distinguishes himself from other men" exploits not social conditions but the individual, the idiosyncratic, the unusual.

Indirect discourse and musical structure are two concepts that Anna Balakian identifies in *The Symbolist Movement* as "constants" of symbolism. The other is the decadent attitude.[4] Baudelaire's contribution to the decadent aesthetic was a combination of scorn for middle-class values, a belief in the superior sensibility, and a sense of the reality of good and evil. His disdain for the mass of mankind was the result of its failure to confront the reality of evil, preferring instead platitudes or evasion. Baudelaire had little faith in conventional assertions of moral progress or social meliorism. In his view human beings were imprisoned by their physical nature, and they suffered as a result of the perpetual conflict between human spirit and physical being. "Le Crépuscule du Matin" portrays this conflict: "When under the body's reluctant, stubborn weight / The soul, like the lamp, renews its unequal fight."[5] The decadent, the superior sensibility, confronted this conflict, preferring to do evil and to suffer than to exist by evasion, that is, by restraining or denying physical nature through moral timidity while projecting guilt upon others.

Baudelaire and Rémy de Gourmont arrived at similar views regarding man's essential nature. Both insisted that man live in conformity with his physical nature rather than shape himself to the dictates of social or religious conventions. Gourmont dismissed Christian doctrines because he felt they dictated that man must deny his physical nature, namely, his sexuality, in order to be truly human. For Gourmont what was essential was recognition that man was an animal. Both Gourmont and Baudelaire recognized that the demands of physical nature, including sexuality, were essential to identity and that denial was destructive. From another perspective, recognizing one's nature meant accepting mortality, especially for those symbolists, like Gourmont, who rejected religious transcendence.

One of Gourmont's most important contributions to the decadent composite was his philosophy of idealism, which, indebted to Schopenhauer, defined the role of perception in shaping reality: "the world (all that is exterior to the self) exists only as the idea formed of it." Reality, then, is always a product of perception. This principle Gourmont described as "the universal principle of emancipation for all men capable of understanding." The task for the writer, consequently, "must be not only the reflection, but the enlarged reflection, of his personality. The only excuse a man has for writing is to write himself—to reveal to others the kind of world reflected in his individual mirror. His only excuse is to be original."[6] Thus, Gourmont's reality and that of the symbolists differs substantially from the naturalists' acceptance of external reality.

Even though creating an "enlarged reflection" of the "world reflected" in an "individual mirror" often led to obscurity and complexity, both were justified, in Gourmont's view, because symbolist art intended "to establish what it can of the eternal in the personal."[7] This aesthetic necessarily resulted in a writer's exploitation of private symbols and experience to convey universal ideas, a practice that was not at all intended to achieve a representational view of reality, although such a view might reflect reality in the same way that Spenser's *Faerie Queen* may be recognized as presenting the reality of moral endeavor.

The values and concepts of symbolism grew from a spirit of rejection: if symbolist writers rejected naturalism's emphasis on the common man or themes common to all men, they focused on extraordinary sensibilities attempting to escape a mundane and vulgar world; if they rejected the revelation of a life as an organizing principle, they turned to idea as a principle to organize the novel's contents. They devised techniques not only to attack a middle-class world view but also to develop the liberating potential inherent in idealism: they avoided direct statement; they used objects, situations, and private symbols to achieve indirect discourse and suggestion. They exploited specifically the "unusual word, object, landscape"; they used "the coupling of abstract and concrete characteristics whose relationship is not ascertained." They preferred the thematic repetition of musical structure, or juxtaposed words or ideas in place of linear, narrative progression. These techniques were intended to "raise the limited experience of man the poet and man the reader to a level of multiple possibilities."[8] They were designed to force a new kind of consciousness. Such an aesthetic demanded from the reader vigilance and reconstruction of meaning: the reader as collaborator.

Barnes's familiarity with symbolists and their ideas can be demonstrated by many references in her early work. The subtitle of one drama (published in *The New York Morning Telegraph* in 1917) points to Baudelaire's influence: "The Death of Life; 'Death Is the Poor Man's Purse—' Baudelaire." Barnes's *A Passion Play* (1918) also reflects Baudelaire's morality. Comments in reviews and letters indicate that Barnes was familiar with the work of other writers whose careers had been influenced by symoblist ideas, including Hauptmann, Hofmannsthal, Maeterlinck, Yeats, and Synge. Allusions in *The Dove* and *Three From the Earth* hint Barnes's familiarity with translations of the writings of symbolist aesthetician Rémy de Gourmont. In February 1919, when Barnes was publishing many of her own works in *The Little Review*, an issue was devoted to Gourmont, who had died in 1915. The tribute attests to the importance of his ideas for many young writers like Barnes.

In placing Barnes's work against the background of symbolism, I have gone against claims that her vision is naturalistic. Although naturalism and symbolism share certain elements, the dominant features of her work point to symbolism as the most appropriate context. Barnes's use of character and plot show that the "delineation of everyday existence," which J.-K. Huysmans pointed to as the limitation of naturalist theory, held little interest for her. Though her characters are sometimes members of the lower social classes, they are presented in situations charged with such tension that they seem extraordinary, heightened, fantastic. They are one-dimensional beings absorbed in the universal problem of identity. Barnes's pervasive interest in the superior sensibility points also to symbolism, rather than naturalism, as the tradition that nourished her early work.

Furthermore, Barnes deliberately rebelled against naturalist techniques. In her fiction Barnes focuses narrowly on a specific moment or limited frame of time. Her concentration in the short stories on a particular incident with virtually no development of story line or character suggests her objection to linear development. In the novel *Ryder*, for example, where we might expect development over time in a naturalistic fashion, Barnes deliberately breaks narrative continuity. She uses repetition of situation and parallel characters to achieve a comic broadness. The organization of *Ryder* emphasizes thematic relationships rather than narrative progression.

In short, Barnes's early fiction demonstrates the heritage of symbolism. She satirizes middle-class values and beliefs. Using techniques of indirection, she achieves meaning by juxtaposing scenes or symbols with little authorial comment. Her characters are stylized, that is, representations of an idea rather than rounded realistic figures. She uses musical structure, which deliberately suppresses narrative movement. Her prose is ambiguous, in places indeterminate.

In approaching Barnes's work from the perspective of symbolist ideas and assumptions, there is no intent to reduce her work to a demonstration of symbolist practices. Naming the heritage and considering its features offer a point of departure. Because Djuna Barnes's work has been considered to be intensely private and autobiographical, if not also eccentric and outside all traditions or allied uneasily with various traditions, an examination of her work from a consistent perspective establishes the wholeness of her work and its artistry.

From the earliest interviews to the jewel-like orchestration of *Ladies Almanack*, Barnes's writing demonstrates increasing sophistication in technique and her persistent concern with what she referred to as "decay," or "the psychological disturbance of the human being to his own nature."[9] Consciousness itself is a theme almost obsessively important to Barnes. Only consciousness seems an ultimate value to Barnes—and even then she saw consciousness as a burden achieved at some cost and with varying degrees of success.

At its best Barnes's early work lives up to the spirit of "avant-garde," or experimental writing, that John Hawkes elaborated in a 1964 interview: the "constant" of experimental writing in his view is a quality

> . . . of coldness, detachment, ruthless determination to face up to the enormities of ugliness and potential failure within ourselves and in the world around us, and to bring to this exposure a savage or saving comic spirit and the saving beauties of language. The need is to maintain the truth of the fractured picture; to expose, ridicule, attack, but always to create and to throw into new light our potential for violence and absurdity as well as for graceful action.[10]

1
Who Is Lydia?

In 1950 Barnes wrote Dan Mahoney, an old friend and the model for Doctor O'Connor of *Nightwood*, that she considered her magazine prose "utterly wasteful."[1] As late as 1977 her attitude remained unchanged, for she refused permission for publication of a collection of *Theatre Guild* pieces, referring to them as the "bottom of the barrel."[2] However, Barnes's journalism is valuable: the essays and interviews from the *New York Morning Telegraph*, from various twenties' journals like *Charm* and *Vanity Fair,* and later from the *Theatre Guild* span the most active period of her fiction writing career, from 1917 to 1929. Thus, the journalism provides a background for the early fiction and supplies examples of her critical principles, the latter particularly apparent in the *Theatre Guild* pieces. What clues to Barnes's fiction are offered in the journalism?

Two traditions dominate Barnes's journalistic writing: decadence, which is related to symbolism, and a concurrent impulse that is satirical. The impetus of each tradition differs. The focus of the symbolist tradition is the individual's attempt to discover satisfactory ways of living, ways that do not deny the human spirit. Within this context Barnes examined individual integrity in a world hostile to it. Less psychological, or individual, in direction, her satire is more social in emphasis. Like most satirists, Barnes admitted to a reforming purpose: "We would teach man with a joke."[3] Consistent with both traditions, Barnes's journalism demonstrates the decadent attitudes that remained with her throughout her life: criticism of American middle-class vulgarity and devotion to art. She saw art as something that transcended mortality and the artist as separate—superior to the common man.

In addition, Barnes's journalism demonstrates her interest in what is extraordinary about the people she interviewed. She pursued the unusual idea—for example, noting playwright David Belasco's collection of items from antiquity and actress Helen Westley's eccentric dress. Perhaps most significant in terms of her later work is the double perspective she experienced: she was a reporter of a culture but also an outsider to the culture she observed. Because she had to reach an audience that she frequently criticized, her journalism often reveals double levels of meaning; an objective view is presented, while she also indirectly raised questions about that view.

Newspaper Journalism: 1913–1922

Barnes's earliest journalism was written for *Bruno's Weekly* and the *Morning Telegraph,* a newspaper that prided itself on being the "Greatest Amusement and Dramatic Publication in the World." These interviews and features reflect Barnes's criticism of middle-class values and her consistent identification with the artist's point of view. In one, for example, she observed that the public attended plays "night after night with mink-trimmed minds and seal-edged morals."[4] In another, she charged a theatre crowd at Provincetown with "killing time, not cultivating it." The play itself? "It had one value only. It was typical of the soul of everything American, the hurry, the ostentation, and the vulgarity."[5]

In an interview with Alfred Stieglitz Barnes threw a baleful glance at the public that regarded art as a kind of uplifting pastime: They were "great droning bores, like buzzards" . . . or "murky women who hover, in casual life, over rare editions of Emerson, Longfellow, and Riley. . . . Or fat ladies burdened with small dogs . . . who say they 'adore' all 'trends,' it is such a great thing for 'progress,' " or worse, "the tourist type, the willowy young man with the pliant cane, and the young women who exclaim enthusiastically, 'What conception of line and color.' "[6]

In the feature "The Hem of Manhattan," Barnes's scorn is withering as passengers in "gingham and dimity gowns" on a boat tour of Manhattan hoped the "educational parts of New York . . . would be visible to the naked eye." Barnes remarked drily, "Well, they were, but they didn't see it. . . . The only refuse that cannot be renovated seems to be the human mind."[7] Her comment derides those young women who represent a trained innocence that denies what is painful. Earlier in "Le chemin de velours" (1901) Gourmont had pointed out the negative effects of the cult of the young lady on literature and argued that the values associated with her—"resignation, modesty, obedience, the sentiment of duty, and an innumerable array of virtues"—falsified human nature and produced sterile writing which was championed by the middle class. "It is for the young 'lady' that the sad novels of Comming and Wood have been translated; for her that the old anthologies have been transformed into manuals of morality . . . for her that *Madame Bovary* was persecuted . . . for her that subsidized theaters emasculate Shakespeare. . . ."[8]

By contrast, the artist's life, or the life of the superior sensibility, is fuller because that life denies neither pain nor the life of the senses. Many of Barnes's interviews focus specifically on the artist's life: How is the artist to live? Should an artist marry? Invariably the answer to the first question is to observe life, usually the life of the streets and the sidewalks: life under pressure. In an interview with Barnes, playwright David Belasco advises:

> Talk with the street girl, talk with the girl of the convent; talk with the baker, talk with the king; go to the roots; examine the flower, be not contemptuous of that community of common particles that unites the highest and the lowest—the stem. Be conscious always; be alert; have eyes and use them; have ears and train them; have a tongue and speak little. If you cultivate your silence your ultimate sounds will be profitable.[9]

The second question, whether the artist should love, regularly evoked a denial that one may have two passions in life.[10] Belasco maintains that an actress "cannot both love a man and her art at the same time. It is impossible! It is suicide." Stieglitz too observes, "One should not be in love; it prevents work and cool, logical study one should love [*sic*]."[11] Each implies that the artist's life is to be lived for the work of art; in other words, the life serves the art.

Stieglitz's comment is followed by a rather peculiar meditation on Barnes's part that relates to the artist's role:

> And I thought: From the place I have been standing eternally, looking out toward the world with my eyes and seeing men pass and look back at me, and I cold and lonesome and increasing steadily in mine own sorrow, which is caught like the plague of other men, until I am full and my mouth will hold no more, and my eyes will see no more, and my ears can stand nothing further, then do I begin the steady, slow discharge which is called "wisdom," but which is only that too much the eyes cannot see, the ears cannot hear, the mouth cannot hold.

The reverie is ended abruptly by her next question, "And so your life from day to day?" The passage and the question draw together two kinds of time, daily time in the latter and timeless experience in the former, and evoke an ageless being who observes life's sorrow and expresses timeless wisdom existing beyond the senses. The personal reverie points to the role of the artist and to Barnes's identification with that role.

In a similar passage, which interrupts a feature on Bohemian life, Barnes exploits concreteness coupled with abstraction to achieve a concept of the poet's task to perceive, or to decipher a reality which is not limited to present conditions:

> And the fan keeps blowing through the world, winnowing the wheat from the chaff. And because the chaff is lighter, it blows up and up and turns and shines in the sun, dancing a moment a mad wild dance—a dance that turns the gaze from the grain lying in a fruitful heap. But the chaff dances slower and slower, down, down and down—it blows out of sight—it has never been. [12]

Once the heightened or personal reality (the wheat) has been perceived and expressed by the artist, it stands as an indictment of transient life (chaff), that is, life limited to present conditions. In contrast to the the limited span and meaning of the individual's life, the artist's work lasts. Barnes's eye seems set, even at this early date, on the wages of originality: to be remembered.

Barnes's perception of life's transience is emphasized in G. B.'s interview with Barnes in 1919:

> Often I sit down to work at my drawing-board, at my typewriter. All of a sudden my joy is gone. I feel tired of it all because, I think, "What's the use? Today we are, tomorrow dead. We are born and don't know why. We live and suffer and strive, envious or envied. We love, we hate, we work, we admire, we despise . . . why? . . . And we die and no one will ever know that we have been born" [Barnes's ellipses]. [13]

The interviewer insists that this is a mood of pessimism, but Barnes denies it. Her feature on Synge suggests that her answer to mortality and life's tedium is one that she shared with Baudelaire: an escape into art— which is not so much an escape but a transcending of sorrow and reality through the mind's expression of that sorrow. She asks, "Was he [Synge] not building by his pen a Synge that will live always as a man who, if he was not always superlatively original—and he admits many sources—is still a beautiful rhythm—let me say an accent—perhaps it is no more— certainly it is no less." [14]

At the time these articles were written, between 1917 and 1922, Barnes, who was twenty-seven, was concerned with death and permanence. The reason may be traced to the death of Mary Pynes, whom Barnes cared for until she died, or it may reflect an awareness she had grown up with; *Ryder,* which contains autobiographic elements, relates Wendell Ryder's fear of death. In any case, like other decadents, Barnes rested her values in art's permanence. Art is not only a vocation; it is a way of life, a way also of transcending death. While she might in a later *Theatre Guild* article refer to the "impudent need to create," she was possessed by that impudence, that need to assert personal existence."[15]

The idea of the permanence of art is latent in a puzzling interview with noted actor Wilson Mizner and accounts, in part, for the uncertain response the article elicits. The Mizner feature is also interesting because it demonstrates Barnes's interest in the character of the talker and her recognition of the way in which Mizner undermines his own credibility while talking. Barnes uses Mizner as epigrammatic speaker to call into question middle-class attitudes. And through the use of implied parallels Barnes achieves an oblique comment on the question of vocation: journalism or poetry, the timely or the timeless.

Her purpose ostensibly is to interview a noted actor who no longer enjoys public attention, but she uses the occasion to raise the issue of fame and its transience. The opening begins: "With hands outspread in hope of collecting profit, I came into the presence of Wilson Mizner, and therein he threw the tinsel of his wit."[16] "I came into the presence" builds the importance of Mizner, but this impression is contradicted by "tinsel." Its connotations of "showy but empty" undercut any idea of "profit." The article's caption reads: "An Old Actor, the Once Applauded, Who Is Now Less Than the Echo of That Applause." The comment hardly seems complimentary, but it announces Barnes's aims: to point to the ephemeral nature of the actor's art, to the transience of life in general, and perhaps also to comment obliquely on her own career as a journalist. If an actor's career was ephemeral, was the journalist's any less so?

Barnes asks Mizner what he thinks of journalism. His answer: "I have not heard of it. What is it? A sort of paper corpse of reportorial parts of intellectuals?" Mizner's comment implies that the journalist's career is also limited, a "paper corpse." When Barnes brings up poetry, Mizner confesses that he has no use for it. His attitude—"it is all right in its place"—identifies him as typical of the indifferent public and perhaps accounts for her subtle criticism directed toward Mizner.

In effect, Barnes has used Mizner as a foil to register her objections regarding journalism, even though she has chosen journalism as a way of freeing herself from the necessity of pleasing art dealers and critics as Guido Bruno has reported.[17] And she indirectly opposed the journalist to the poet: the timely to the timeless. Barnes thus enjoyed the luxury of "biting the hand that fed her": while she dissociated herself from journalism, she affirmed her vocation as artist.

In the newspaper journalism (1913–22) we find the seeds that come to

fruition in Barnes's later work. Barnes's satire and the decadent tradition
come together in her criticism of middle-class conventions and values,
including the complacency and decorum that produced the "young
lady." Her interest in unusual traits of character and her fascination with
the epigrammatic character seem more closely related to decadent tradition, though the two cannot be easily separated. The epigrammatic
talker, for example, is employed not only as a foil to middle-class values
but also as a figure of self-deception and thus is related to decadence
with its concern for individual integrity. Barnes's decadence is apparent
also in her awareness of mortality and her devotion to art—concerns that
appear to be motivated, at least in part, by her sense of personal transience. In addition, Barnes demonstrated her inclination for indirect
communication; by identifying with a figure like Mizner while subtly
questioning his values, she created ripples of double meaning. Between
1922 and 1928 Barnes continued to explore satire and the decadent
tradition and to address the question of vocation raised in the Mizner
feature.

Magazine Journalism: 1922–1928

Around 1922 Barnes joined the expatriates in Paris. During these years
Barnes's uneasiness with her journalistic career becomes more apparent,
perhaps because she was beginning to experience success with her
serious work. In October 1923 *A Book* appeared, her first collection of
fiction, poetry, drama, and drawings.[18] Furthermore, during the latter
half of this decade, from December 1924 until the 1928 appearance of
Ryder and the 1929 publication of *A Night among the Horses*, Barnes
appears to have devoted less time to her journalistic work and more time
to her serious fiction.

However, when Barnes first went to Paris, it was to report on expatriate life for *McCall's*. Primarily journalistic, many of these pieces bore the
pseudonym, Lydia Steptoe, which Barnes began to use in August 1922.
Louis F. Kannenstine has suggested that Barnes began to write magazine
journalism to broaden her audience, but Barnes's adoption of Lydia
Steptoe as a pseudonym at this time casts doubt on this explanation.
Furthermore, the reading public of *Vanity Fair* and *Charm* was not the
public Barnes wished to appeal to. The articles she wrote for these
publications dealt primarily with fashion: clothing, jewelry, and important French designers. A reasonable surmise is that magazine writing
gave her both more money and freedom for the kind of writing she
wanted to do. An article like "American Wives and Titled Husbands"
brought five hundred dollars; few who wrote for a living passed by such

opportunities—and Barnes was one of the expatriate crowd who was not blessed with an independent income.[19] Given the success of her serious writing, the adoption of a pseudonym may have satisfied a desire to separate the two careers.

Barnes's magazine journalism was of two kinds. She interviewed famous people, usually associated with theatre or fashion, and she created satiric sketches that were often signed by Lydia Steptoe. Between 1922 and 1924 the pieces that carried Lydia Steptoe's name did not vary in tone, attitude, or subject matter from other pieces written during this time that were signed by Barnes. For example, Barnes signed the sketch, "Two Ladies Take Tea" (*Shadowland,* April 1923), which is similar to the September 1922 *Vanity Fair* piece, "Little Drops of Rain," signed by Lydia. The pseudonym was also used for direct reporting, such as "A French General of Fashion," and "A French Couturiere to Youth."[20] A similar style of article from *Charm,* "The Models Have Come to Town," appeared slightly earlier in November 1924 and carried Barnes's name. Even a serious piece of reporting on the Little Theaters of Rome (August 1926) carried the pen name Lydia Steptoe. Thus, in the magazine prose published between 1922 and 1924, Barnes's signature and the pen name appeared to be interchangeable.

After December 1924, however, the pen name was used exclusively for magazine journalism with the exception of two 1925 *McCall's* articles. One of these articles was an interview with D. W. Griffith, and the other an interview with famous American women who had married titled European husbands. One may speculate, then, that between 1924 and 1925 Barnes determined to devote herself to a career as a serious artist and chose to assign virtually all magazine work, whether serious or satirical, to Lydia Steptoe.

Lydia, as a precocious girl who-would-be-liberated, not only satirized the cult of the pure "young lady" but also continued Barnes's fascination with the epigrammatic talker. Just as the talker in the Mizner feature undermined himself, or was undermined by the author, so too Lydia's would-be sophistication was open to genial criticism. On another level, the creation of Lydia Steptoe perhaps served private purposes as well. Barnes and Lydia shared a charm and a witty gregariousness. For example, Barnes's comment on her return to the United States contained a hint of the chatty gaiety of Lydia: "What you save, you spend on clothes."[21] As heiress to Barnes's journalistic success, Lydia represented elements of personality that Barnes eventually rejected, just as she also rejected journalism as detrimental to her art.

Despite Barnes's disavowal of them, the magazine pieces are interesting because they continue the satiric tradition of her early newspaper work, providing a sample of the humor that is carried into the one-acts but that is less evident in the short stories of the same period. While the criticism of the newspaper sketches had been centered on the middle class and its assumptions, the satiric sketches from the Paris years demonstrate Barnes's concern with the forces of convention and identity. Most of these pieces focus specifically on women's identity. "Against Nature," for example, is one of several satirical sketches that satirizes the "young lady": "I hate the jeune fille. There isn't that much youth. They are always exclaiming 'Where am I?' when they wake up a little too early for breakfast."[22]

Lydia's comic tirade includes the Victorian veneration for motherhood:

> Now what I want to know is why babies are considered such justifiers of a woman's existence?
> To justify yourself more than five or six times in a life is rather insisting on the point, it seems to me; a point that even Nature would drop—and Nature almost never drops a point.
> Yet some women go right on to the seventh or eighth.
> I think it would be far more delicate of women, in every way, to stop clinching arguments with children.
> Womanhood should not be thrust upon the attention. (P. 60)

When Lydia questions "why babies are considered such justifiers of a woman's existence," she reveals her impatience with traditional concepts of a woman's role; being a woman was an aspect of one's identity, an identity that existed without the justification of children; indeed, she mocks "Nature" to assert the point.

"The Diary of a Dangerous Child" presents the quandary young women faced when they realized the limitations of middle-class expectations. In this piece, developed in diary form, the heroine examines her choices: "I am debating with myself whether I shall place myself in some good man's hands and become a mother, or if I shall become a wanton and go out in the world and make a place for myself." She considers what it will mean to her father, "who is a lawyer," and to her mother, "who is in society," concluding, "I should be an idiot for their sakes." The heroine's penultimate diary entry humorously reveals the resolution of her dilemma: "Yes, I have quite changed my mind. I am neither going to give myself into the hands of some good man, and become a mother, nor am I going to go out in the world and become a wanton. I am going to run away and become a boy."[23] The decision to "become a boy" represents the precocious girl's desire to participate in a world wider than social convention allowed. Huck could go West to escape conventions that stifled his individuality, but a woman had to become somebody else.

Several of Lydia's pieces spoof middle-class expectations and docility through the form of etiquette advice. "What Is Good Form in Dying?" satirizes those who shape their lives according to social codes:

> One must die in good taste. Yet how many people fail to realise that there is a ritual of good form for death as there is for life!
> . . . Heavy tomes have been compiled on the art of living; mail order houses do a rushing business issuing sample letters of love, rejection, and despair. . . . but where, I ask you, is there one single thin, succint, touching, ineluctable brochure on death, and the correct manner in which a young lady may die?
> No, these things have been, for countless centuries, left to the inspiration of the moment. No wonder people drag on dreary and inappropriate lives, rather than lay themselves open to adverse comment by their ignorance of good form in dying.[24]

Lydia enumerates appropriate and tasteful deaths—according to hair color. She cautions the blond woman against "the social error of choosing an unbecoming and unromantic death by shooting." Instead, "She should hang, preferably, from some frail Early Italian object. . . ." The red-haired woman—Barnes had auburn hair—should die by water, but Lydia concludes that "it's hard to make them do it." They prefer ways "just as good as death"—seclusion or countless activities. The comment is tantalizing, for it captures Barnes's career precisely.

In this essay, satire is directed at the idea of "good taste" as the appropriate value in life, and at the idea that the art of living is a matter of writing proper letters and attracting successful suitors. The "people who drag on dreary and inappropriate lives" are thus identified with those who live according to form, those who are afraid to "lay themselves open to adverse comment."

Though some of Barnes's female characters attempt to escape conventional lives, most lack self-knowledge or the will to create a more satisfactory life. In these sketches Barnes's humor is directed not only toward middle-class values but also toward the heroine whose escape from convention is often thwarted by her own weaknesses. In the "Diary of a Dangerous Child" the young girl intends to outwit convention and her mother by electing to escape via "the dangerous marriage." She arranges to meet her sister's suitor, Don Passos Dilemma. However, the cloaked figure at the garden gate turns out to be her mother. In effect, the deception suggests that the mother perpetuates her own victimization through her daughter. She enforces the code of purity and safe marriage while opposing the daughter's assertion of her own identity, that is, "going out and becoming wanton."

In "The Beauty," satire is focused on a woman who tires of being wooed in the same "old custom" of false avowals. She wishes to be treated as an equal: "I have allowed myself to be degraded by the spectacle of a man who calls admiration for a pretty face love. . . . The man I marry must . . . take me as an equal."[25] But when confronted by a student who proposes to disregard her beauty and treat her as an equal, she seeks out her former lover.

A similar example is nineteen-year-old Mitzi Ting of "Little Drops of Rain": "I won't conserve. I want to abandon myself to live fully—."[26] She thinks she has chosen the dangerous, eccentric life by marrying Sir Horace Droop, a man with whom her aunt, Lady Lookover, has had a dalliance. In fact, given Sir Horace Droop's name and Lady Lookover's prediction that Mitzi is fit for nothing but a safe marriage, readers recognize that Sir Horace Droop is but one aspect of the conventional dilemma: Mitzi can become wanton or married. In choosing Sir Horace Droop, she has betrayed her desire for an unconventional life.

In the magazine journalism of the Paris years, between 1922 and 1928, Barnes integrated her satiric attack on middle-class convention with the theme of personal identity. From Barnes's double perspective, humor was directed not only at social conventions but against self-deluded heroines betrayed by their own vanity or their failure to see the situation properly. Often the desire of these heroines to be independent is merely a pose, a wish to appear unconventional while remaining safely within convention. Thus, Barnes indicates that while women may be victims of social conventions, these conventions are perpetuated by self-deception. Integrity, she implies, is rare.

As we will see in the following chapters, themes of identity and self-deception permeate the fiction of the Paris period. But first let us conclude this overview of Barnes's journalism with a look at the work written for *Theatre Guild* between 1929 and 1931 during Barnes's brief return to America.

Theatre Guild Magazine: 1929–1931

After 1929 most of Barnes's journalism appeared in *Theatre Guild,* and all of it, except for a single piece attributed to Lady Lydia Steptoe, appeared under her own name. Even though she used her own name, she did not regard this work as serious, referring to it as the "bottom of the barrel." The work consisted of a monthly series called "Playgoer's Almanac," which gave way in 1931 to "Wanton Playgoer." Both series with their snippets of ideas have a gossip column quality: "Remarque's *All Quiet on the Western Front* has made him so much Trouble (it is a political Issue in Berlin and Austria) that he has become not so worry that he *went* to the War, as he is that he *told* on It."[27]

More important are the monthly features devoted to theatre: a retrospective look at Provincetown, articles featuring prominent playwrights like Rachel Crothers and scene designers like Jo Mielziner and Mordecai Gorelik. Though many of these articles touch regularly upon negative aspects of society and culture, they are less important for their social criticism than for the light that they shed on Barnes's artistic ideas and practices. These works are particularly important because of their position in Barnes's career; they cap her journalistic career and provide insights into the creative activity of the previous decade, one which saw the completion of *Ryder, Ladies Almanack,* several one-acts, and many of the short stories that were collected first in *A Book* (1923) and later in *A Night among the Horses* (1929). In short, this work demonstrates Barnes's continuing concern with identity and provides evidence not available elsewhere of her critical thinking.

Barnes's preoccupation with human striving and identity is expressed in a December 1929 *Theatre Guild* piece in which ingenuous Brother Sumac questions the nature of human identity. He observes that actors "when they reach fifty . . . do not remember what they were, but what Hamlet said." He implies that actors are a peculiarly apt representation of human nature—a collection of roles, parts played—rather than an established identity with a consistent morality. In this fictitious dialogue between Brother Sumac and a "noted" actress, Brother Sumac (sounding very much like the Matthew O'Connor of *Nightwood*) is worried by the "passion in the human heart to be something it is not," and he points out the ambiguous nature of the desire: he is "not sure if it is a true aspiration or a terrible and unholy criticism of the Most High." He confesses that though he himself wants to be good, he has been "fashioned exceedingly evil."[28] Sumac thus raises one of the central questions of Barnes's work: what is the truth of human nature and how are we to know? A partial answer is implicit in Barnes's drama criticism.

Primarily what Barnes objected to in contemporary theatre was its lack of moral concern—and its literalness. In "Dear Dead Days," there was no sympathetic nod to youthful rebellion. Instead, she criticized the play *Young Love* because she found no consciousness of moral issues:

> We are horrified, legitimately and historically so, when we see a young girl going against convention and in the going suffering neither remorse, rich increase, pleasure in "falling," nor advancement. When she picks herself up she does not even brush turpitude off her gown.[29]

Despite losses in terms of moral certainty, she approved in the contemporary situation a rejection of Victorian codes that were destructive of woman's identity; she concluded that "it is far better than that one Bronte should be sacrificed to the brother, which was traditional when love was love, and sin was sin and never the two could mix and mingle. Sin led to Hades, and love to a lot of male children doted upon by a mother who bore a sufficient number of girls to clean up after them." Elsewhere in the same article Barnes asserted that a definite standard was necessary for a general public—but that artists "will always do as they please." In doing so, she assumes an ethical norm that is self-generated by superior sensibilities, who are conscious of the gains and losses of defying a code. Such a view implies that individual consciousness can raise human conduct above the level of physical instinct.

This view of human nature is related to "decay," a concept central to her aesthetics. Both decay and pretense, another concept related to technique, are introduced in a feature on set designer, Mordecai Gorelik. In the Gorelik feature Barnes referred to a dramatic production as an "elastic hour in which decay (or the psychological disturbances of the human being to his own nature) has also its measure of fruition." Thus, "decay" implies a person's coming to consciousness, that is, recognizing "his own nature."[30] Her objection to contemporary theatre was that it evaded this consciousness. We remember that years earlier in a *Telegraph* feature Barnes had attacked both audience and play for the same kind of evasion.

In "The Tireless Rachel Crothers," Barnes's faint praise damns Crothers by associating her with middle-class mediocrity and provincialism. Her technique is similar to the veiled undercutting she had used in the Mizner feature years earlier. Her headline and subhead announce negative implications: Crothers is "tireless"; her twenty-fourth play is another in her "long and methodical career." Crothers herself is described as having "that stubborn look; a little woman with white hair, fan shaped over the ears, close set misty eyes, a slightly receding chin offset by a mouth nipped in at the corners—a person who will listen, but who will not change her mind."[31]

One can imagine that Barnes, who had failed to place her own play, was irritated by Crothers's assurance that "Everyone receives the attention which he deserves, everyone gets a chance sooner or later. I do not believe there are any masterpieces in oblivion, anyway no plays." To Barnes's objections that *Green Pastures* was produced only as a last gesture, "a sort of wholesale farewell, a goodbye in the grand manner," and that Pirandello had never received the acclaim he deserved, Mrs. Crothers is quoted as saying, "Ah yes, that strange fellow from Italy—" Barnes, in confessing that she had seen only the last of Crothers's twenty-five plays, essentially dismissed her: "from its tone I gather that all were light, amusingly handled, dealing with the social problem of the moment, rather than that of the race." From the comment's tone, we may assume that Barnes preferred literary work that reached beyond "social problems of the moment."

What Barnes desired was work that grasped the issues of the race, presumably the issues of morality and mortality. What was lacking was "The will-to-see-things-through with the mind." Indicative of the present mentality was the demand for stage realism, literal representation at the expense of imaginative realization. In the one essay of this period credited to Lydia Steptoe, Barnes objected to the destruction of props to convey emotion on the stage. As Lydia observed, "When you cut down on man's ingenuity you pep up wreckage of inanimate objects."[32] Literalness and stage realism thus usurped the role of imagination.

Behind this objection to stage realism was the second principle of her own aesthetic practice: pretense. In her feature on scene designer Raymond Sovey she described the shortcoming of realism as a lack of imaginative energy that revitalized old themes: "that 'something' else— that magic re-iteration of a past that makes of an old statement a new wonderment and a new reality—this will be missing."[33] And in the feature on Mordecai Gorelik, she distinguished between "illusion," or "the effort to make a bedroom look exactly like a bedroom," and "pretense," which is "the effort to suggest the bedroom with the cooperation of the spectator." She elaborated the aim of pretense:

> Pretense gives the bedroom a chance to be imaginative, to be personal, as a human being is personal in not being an exact copy of another human being. This can, at times, be approximated by going intentionally, but feelingly, against the grain of the living emotion about to be acted on the stage; it gives the whole a relatively accurate tempo through an orchestration that is dissimilar but in keeping, the problem of the theatre being the bringing to harness of as many chords as can be appropriated to one theme, some parts swift, others slow.[34]

Barnes's comment—as well as her musical metaphor—is intriguing with respect to her own work, for it affirms her disinclination to explore representational realism in favor of achieving a kind of reality through the active relationship of observer (or reader) and materials presumed to be contrasting and various in nature. While Barnes defined "pretense" in the context of stage scenery, the term can be extended. When she refers to "going intentionally, but feelingly against the grain of the living emotion about to be acted on the stage," she affirms the power of contrasting moods. Some idea of what she intends may be seen in "Just

Getting the Breaks," an interview with Donald Ogden Stewart where contrasting emotions are used humorously to criticize middle-class banality.

In this interview Barnes set herself up as a foil to Stewart's success: his careless exuberance contrasts with her resignation and sense of failure:

> "See here," we said darkly, "do you realize that you and I started together as it were. That you were tiptoeing out of Crowninshield's office about the same hour that we were creeping in, and are we on Broadway? Do you know that good looking women, with yards and yards of golden hair and all that, have paid, and paid, and paid, to be where you are, and are still paying, off stage? . . . Do you," we suddenly shouted, frenzied with blighted hopes, and maddened with years of living through the darkness before the dawn, "do you ever think of those millions who have trained, and struggled, and wept, just to attain to a certain well merited oblivion, while you, without so much as a smothered sob, roll over and find yourself famous, and not only that but appear before the public, night after night, and get a hand?"

To his witty rejoinder, "What's the matter? In need of money?", Barnes replies, "Oh no, we interview successful people just to prevent ourselves from becoming groggy with rich port and caviar; to save ourselves from becoming blunted with idleness, to arm ourselves against doing murder to one or more of our slaves and outrunners!"[35] The exaggeration, of course, is funny; the tip-off rests in the heavy emphasis on "paid and paid and paid" and on the clichés "frenzied with blighted hope," and "darkness before the dawn."

She closes the interview, accentuating again the difference between Stewart and herself: "We looked at him a long moment, standing right in the middle of the spotlight of fame as the shadows of oblivion crept up to our chins." She asks the question that is often repeated in her earlier journalistic pieces:

> "Do you want to die?"
> "No," he answered lightly, "do you?"
> "We don't mind," we answered, stepping into the night.

Despite the comic exaggeration, the ending is too stark to allow a reader much comic relief. The contrasting moods of comedy and the exaggerated bitterness seem intended to achieve a purging effect, mocking cultural values and mocking self as well. In much the same way Barnes had created Lydia Steptoe as heiress of her journalistic reputation and success, then separated herself from that persona while drolly attacking Lydia's superficiality. Here, however, the desired balance between comedy and bitterness is tenuous. Beneath the self-mockery, the hint of frustration comes through with unnerving clarity.

As important as pretense to Barnes's critical thinking is her concept of "multiple chords." She states: "the problem of the theatre being the bringing to harness of as many chords as can be appropriated to one theme." The implications of "multiple chords," or ideas related to a central theme, are most clearly demonstrated in her own work by *Ryder* and *Ladies Almanack,* whose forms, as we shall see in following chapters, achieve the effect of multiple chords.

Barnes's journalism reveals many of the assumptions that pervade her work. While much of the early newspaper work is satirical, it also establishes her affinity with symbolist attitudes, including its criticism of middle-class complacency, provincialism, and materialism, and its emphasis on individual consciousness. The *Theatre Guild* essays, the one-acts, and the short fiction that she wrote throughout her journalistic career demonstrate that she succeeded not only in making these ideas her own but also in establishing her own voice while she did so.

While Barnes spent many years as a newspaper and magazine journalist, she had early set her sights on issues more important than the passing moments and had determined to do more than amuse. Thus, it must have seemed ironic to her that the serious work she wished to do was not well received, but the journalism that came so easily and that she scorned was applauded.[36] Though Barnes would have liked her serious work to be recognized by a public capable of accepting it, she resolved as other artists had done before her that a fit but small audience was preferable to a vast audience acquired by artistic compromise. She wrote newspaper and magazine journalism to survive, but she did not value it.

2
On the Road to Provincetown

In *The Magic Curtain* Lawrence Langner wrote that the plays of Djuna Barnes "combined a startling sense of dramatic values with an incoherence of expression that made everything she wrote exciting and baffling at the same time."[1] Both complimentary and yet slightly negative, the comment is typical of the kind of perplexity that Barnes's drama elicited from the very beginning.

Most of Barnes's one-acts appeared between 1916 and 1923, during the later part of her newspapers career and into the Paris years of the magazine journalism. Thus, her drama shares with the early newspaper journalism its intention to confront the public of "mink-trimmed minds" and "seal-edged morals" and with the magazine work of the Paris years its concern with identity, in particular woman's identity. Most of these one-acts were published in various magazines or newspapers like *Others* or the *Morning Telegraph*.

Two concepts articulated in a 1931 *Theatre Guild* essay, specifically "decay" and "pretense," are useful in discussing Barnes's methods in these plays. In her feature on Mordecai Gorelik, Barnes defined *decay* as "the psychological disturbances of the human being to his own nature." The idea implies the individual's coming to conscious recognition of his nature or the significance of that nature. The concept necessarily focuses attention on the individual, though not as a member of a social group or as a victim of social pressures or hereditary forces.

Pretense and its implications are more complex, and they involve the spectator.[2] Barnes seems to see pretense and imagination as related concerns which can be used to contrast "the living emotion about to be acted on the stage." As an example she cites Gorelik's use of caricature in scene design "when the original mood of the play became too sentimen-

34

tal or self-pitying for a modern audience." In addition, her definition of the problem of the stage as a matter of orchestration of chords suggests that one of her aims is to deny simple rational perception in order to create a complex and deliberate form of communication that disrupts traditional expectations. Such methods demand that the reader or audience give in to the process of re-forming expectations and opinions. Barnes's plays reinforce this tendency by using a sudden twist or an opaque conclusion to force disoriented viewers to reasses expectations and to look for new patterns or perspectives that are consistent with the play's conclusion.

Few of Barnes's plays present an easily discernible meaning, but the first group is generally accessible, with the possible exception of *At the Root of the Stars* and *Passion Play*. These early plays reflect Barnes's pervasive concern with human nature and with social conditions faced by the artist. In *Death of Life, At the Root of the Stars*, and *Kurzy of the Sea*, the artist, or a figure identified as apart from daily concerns, is beset by middle-class attitudes and confronted with mortality. In *An Irish Triangle* and *Passion Play* Barnes focuses on middle-class morality; *Passion Play*, in particular, is concerned with morality and repression. In this group only *Kurzy of the Sea* and *An Irish Triangle* were performed; the others appeared in the *Telegraph* or in various little magazines.

A second and more successful group of plays—*To the Dogs, Three from the Earth*, and *The Dove*—explore sexual repression, exploiting a literal level and demanding that viewers reach for a level of implication beyond the surface. Certainly these plays were intended to challenge conventional morality, particularly with respect to sexuality. All of Barnes's plays touch on sexuality and social conformity as related forces of personal identity. Wherever the individual's sexuality is compromised by social codes, identity itself is betrayed.

In the first group of plays, which deals with the superior sensibility and with middle-class values, Barnes seems satisfied with direct exposition of ideas spoken by characters rather than developed by action. Barnes uses an Irish dialect in several of these plays, though discovering why she did so is problematic. The use may suggest the influence of Synge. Barnes had written in a *Morning Telegraph* appreciation that "Synge first touched the Irish in me." She admired his Irish rhythm, but added in a more equivocal vein "so sometimes I also do not want to be awakened from the certain joyous blindness that was Synge's."[3] The emphasis here must be on *sometimes*, for Barnes's work as a whole reveals a persistent concern with self-deception and conscious awareness. Her preference is accorded to characters who face their nature, though she might occasionally play with the theme of self-deception, as she does in the Irish pieces.

The Death of Life: "Death Is the Poor Man's Purse"—Baudelaire explores Baudelaire's idea that the soul is weighed down by demands of the body. Specifically, the play is concerned with the artist's livelihood, an issue of special interest to Barnes. In the 21 October 1915 issue of *Bruno's Weekly,* Guido Bruno had reported that Barnes had become a journalist so that she could support herself independent of the demands of publishers and art dealers, thus permitting "herself the luxury of being an artist just to please herself."[4]

In the play, the central character is Ragna, an artist, who faces the fact that "one must sell one's mind often to live at all." Rather than compromise her life as an artist, she kills herself. A friend, who has given up his artistic dreams for a steady job, confirms that her death is a triumph: "Ah, what a fine, proud spirit your's [sic] was girl . . . and it's a fine death you have."[5] The denouement affirms that in taking her life, Ragna has triumphed over the physical being that humbles and betrays the spirit.

Though *The Death of Life* presents Ragna's suicide as a triumph, it also reveals the very fragile nature of her spirit. This theme is treated differently in *At the Root of the Stars* (February 1917). For ten years after her son's departure for the war, Mageen has been a recluse in a basement room of her boardinghouse. Despite the exile she is a vital woman; her laugh "is at once loud and full of pleasure, with an undertone that hints biting sarcasm and bitter wit." When a neighbor questions her seclusion, Mageen affirms: "It's glad I am to be at the roots of the stars, for it's the roots get the truth. The sun coming out for a moment may deceive the flower, but the root knows the lie."[6] The action is built around making those words and their significance concrete.

Mageen spins lovingly the moment of her son's return, asserting her ability to recognize his footstep. Suddenly, she starts, recognizing the footfall she has evoked. She orders the maid to bring him in. The maid returns, however, announcing that she can't bring him in. The footsteps Mageen has heard are those of a donkey. One can imagine the audience's consternation at hearing the maid announce that the footsteps Mageen has heard belong to a donkey, only to watch the final curtain fall. The action is clear enough, but what does it mean?

In the *Theatre Guild* feature on Mordecai Gorelik, written fourteen years later, Barnes referred to "multiple chords" as a contrast to the "living emotion" being acted on the stage. This seems to be the effect she intended in *At the Root of the Stars*. To reconcile the contrast between Mageen's longing and the comic deflation of that longing, the audience has to reconsider what has been experienced; specifically they must consider Mageen's character and the contrast established between the basement setting of Mageen as recluse and the strength and realism of her spirit. In effect, Barnes plays the audience's emotional expectation—a depressing setting—against Mageen's spirited resilience. Mageen's sureness, set against the conclusion's anticlimax, invites the reader to see Mageen as a deluded fool. However, the beauty of her expression, the "rightness" of her demands on life, her pride in "all that life can mean and cannot be," and the bravery of her conception win respect, though reality falls short, for the steps she hears belong to a donkey, not her son.

While Mageen is momentarily deceived, she, unlike Ragna, goes on because her concept of life accommodates both life's possibility and its actuality: the flower and the root. Her retreat has put her in touch with life's essentials, the roots, and that knowledge preserves her even in the face of harsh and ironic reality. Her "bitter wit" is a sign of a tougher spirit than Ragna possesses. Ragna's fragile spirit is threatened by life and is preserved only by death. Mageen, by contrast, represents a tougher spirit which can both conceive a dream and accept its compromise without being threatened.

In *Kurzy of the Sea* (April 1920), Barnes turned again to the superior sensibility's vision of life. In this comedy, the second of Barnes's plays performed by the Provincetown Players, reality lives up to the hero's imaginative conception of it. For viewers (or readers) uncertainty resides in various ways of understanding the conclusion, but the action, on the surface, is resolved. This play allows an audience, who may experience the drama as portraying a boy-gets-girl plot, the luxury of remaining at the surface level of the action. And evidently *Kurzy* lived up to the audience's expectations, for Alexander Woolcott wrote that *Kurzy of the Sea* was a "mildly diverting Djuna Barnes pleasantry which is actually intelligible (possibly through oversight). . . ."[7]

The play has a fairy-tale, tall-tale quality to it. Two attitudes toward life are represented in Rory McRace's demand for the extraordinary and his parents' unquestioning acceptance of the way things are. Rory's "spirited melancholy" opposes mundane reality. Described as "aspiring" and in search of a "fleeting spirit," he frustrates his parents by insisting that he will marry only "a Queen or a Saint or a Venus, or whatever it is comes in with the tide."[8]

Rory's demand for the extraordinary, "a real unhuman woman," seems to be met when his father appears and presents him with a mermaid he has taken from the sea. Rory rides out with her, but returns quickly, announcing that he has thrown Kurzy back into the sea; "And I called out to her: 'Kurzy girl, if you're a saint it's I shall be knowing in a moment, for if you are you'll swim, and if not, you'll drown.' " However, Kurzy's spirited taunting as she swims away wins Rory, who decides that instead of the mare promised by his mother if he marries, "it's a boat I shall be needing" (p. 13).

Though Kurzy is no queen, Venus, or saint, she is no ordinary woman either. Thus, Rory's demand, his dream of life, seems affirmed. However, as Kurzy is revealed to be the barmaid at the White Duck Tavern and therefore human and mortal, perhaps Barnes intends to suggest that we betray our dreams by settling for the superficially attractive reality. If so, the play comments on human capacity for self-deception, a failure to perceive situations accurately. On yet another level, Rory's acceptance of Kurzy may mean that he accepts his own mortality: he accepts his limited nature. The multiple possibilities of the conclusion testify to the various perspectives that accompany any action. While Rory's parents may be pleased, is the audience to assume that he has betrayed his dreams? Or that recognizing humanity is necessarily a betrayal, though there are advantages? The ambiguity itself points to the "fruition of decay": consciousness of mortal nature, which is both a gain and a loss.

An Irish Triangle (December 1920) was the third and last of Barnes's one-acts performed by the Provincetown group. It is the slightest in substance, though Heywood Broun, in reviewing Barnes's play in addition to those by other authors on the evening's bill, had headlined it as the "Best of the New One-Act Pieces." In this play Barnes humorously treats the willingness of a young couple to sacrifice middle-class respectabilty for gain, and she also questions middle-class attitudes by placing the audience in a morally ambivalent situation.[9] The action of the play, unlike the developing plot of *Kurzy*, is Sheila's discovery of the meaning of past actions. Sheila visits her friend Kathleen and unexpectedly finds her calm and happy. Kathleen defends her husband's visits to the manor, a topic of town gossip, because he relates to her the manners and taste of a lady of the upper class. As a final twist, Kathleen indicates that she will visit the the lord of the manor to pass on to John the manners and taste of an upper-class gentleman. Sheila is outraged: "And it's I don't know what to make of you, and the terrible triangle that's come into your life."[10] Sheila voices the moral views of the town, but her eagerness to pass along tales of Kathleen's suffering or to censure her also draws Barnes's satire. Barnes's audience must have felt some consternation to discover that the ambition and sexual trespass of Kathleen and John are untouched by comic censure, which is reserved instead for Sheila's respectability.

The last play in this group is *Passion Play*. Published in *Others* (February 1918), it deals with middle-class morality and repression. Barnes brings together Christian ideas of suffering and redemption and Baudelaire's idea that a man who sins and is conscious of it is closer to redemption than one who denies and projects his sin. This play differs from the rest of Barnes's drama in that it is allegorical. For this reason the play is difficult, but more important, the language is evasive, paradox-ical; words have multiple connotations that remain unfixed. Odor, for example, is a concept that the two thieves and the two prostitutes associate with deviation from social norms, including sexual norms, and with sexuality, death, evil, and health. Theocleia says to the second thief, "You are a dirty ruffian, but I like the odor of your filth, 'tis healthy." Later she comments, "We are to the world what odor is to the flesh—".[11] Readers' views of these characters depend on the extent to which we identify with them, i.e., see them as victims of an inhibited, repressive, and hypocritical society. Or do we, in spite of the thieves' dialogue, identify with the society that has defined them as outcasts?

As evening draws near, the thieves disappear with the prostitutes into the surrounding darkness, but, moments later, when light returns to the stage signaling morning, three crosses, not two, are now visible on the hillside, and the two prostitutes reappear with thirteen pieces of silver—a detail that marks them as betrayers of Christ.

The primary difficulty of the play derives from the juxtaposition of two actions: the thieves' dialogue with the prostitutes and Christ's cru-cifixion which, though suggested only by scenic backdrop, provides the multiple-chords effect Barnes articulated later in the "Mordecai Gorelik" essay. Resolution is difficult because the dialogue and the action seem to contradict one another. The thieves' dialogue has emphasized that though they are social scapegoats, they are not different from other men; they simply live out what others deny. Though outlaws, they are out-laws because of the limited capacities of others: "All people have ap-petites, but few have stomachs" (p. 9).

If recognition of evil brings one closer to repentance, we would expect the play to portray that recognition by the thieves before their crucifixion or after, if only symbolically, by the prostitutes. But this recognition does not occur, apparently denying the Baudelairean idea established in the thieves' dialogue. Though the prostitutes observe a momentary change in the air, a clearing, they return to daily life and gaming for the property the thieves have left. Thus, the play seems to deny the premise upon which it is based. In fact, however, the thieves fail to recognize evil; they refer to how the world sees them, but never to how they see themselves. They are, then, like the world that condemns others while failing to recognize its own guilt.

Their sense of evil allows them a superiority that mirrors the falsely assumed purity of those who condemn them. The play is thus an adroit mirror image of middle-class rationalization and self-righteousness. Whether readers reject or concur in the thieves' view, they find them-selves, more directly than in *An Irish Triangle*, included in a questionable moral community.

The usual pattern in most of the plays of this group is a static situation in which two characters discuss a past event. Only *Kurzy of the Sea* involves some action. While we may conclude that these plays are simply undramatic, we should not overlook the fact that the static quality of the one-acts suggests that Barnes's interest resides in adaptations that characters make to reality and their consciousness in doing so. Often the characters themselves do not realize their situation, but the audience is drawn into the situation because of the baffling effects of various kinds of irony. The opaque conclusion in *At the Root of the Stars,* for example, forces the viewer to reconsider Mageen's character in order to compre- hend the conclusion's significance. Similarly, the ambiguous conclusion of *Kurzy of the Sea* invites one to see an event from different perspectives, all of which are acceptable interpretations of the play's action. The viewer's experience of *An Irish Triangle* is also disarming, for in this play viewers who identify with Sheila find their own values are questioned by humorous elements of the play. *Passion Play,* though very similar to Barnes's overt use of a Baudelairean theme, as seen in *Death of Life,* is Barnes's first dramatic treatment of sexual repression, a theme that drew her best efforts in *To the Dogs, Three from the Earth,* and *The Dove.*

In this second group of plays, Barnes's aim is to capture the interplay of concealment and revelation that results from sexual repression. In each play the situation seems clear, but it does not account for the tension between characters, who spar with one another in oblique and cryptic dialogue. Each play depends therefore on a reader's perception of each character's motives, motives that are often obscured by the dialogue. Barnes's practice suggests not only that characters deceive themselves through language but that language itself is deceptive.

The technique of *To the Dogs* (*A Book,* 1923), like its idea, is similar to that of *Passion Play.* Two ideas are introduced through two kinds of characters; development of characters is not the objective. In contrast to *Passion Play* where overt allegory enables us to spot the ideas readily, the characters in *To the Dogs* are ostensibly realistic, thereby muting symbolic aspects of character.

The play presents the confrontation between Helena Hucksteppe, a woman of thirty-five, and Gheid Storm, a "man of few years." He is "decidedly masculine" and has been raised by "upright women." Louis Kannenstine characterizes Helena Hucksteppe as "another of Miss Barnes' overdrawn women." He regards her "as a finished portrait . . . there is no development. . . ." He adds that Barnes is "unable to sustain much interest in the outcome" of the confrontation between Helena and Storm because "Helena is the victor in sexual supremacy at the outset."[12] Though there is basic antagonism between Helena and Storm, to sub- stitute "between the sexes" for "between Helena and Storm," reduces the play unnecessarily to a male vs. female plot. Instead, the play focuses on two responses to reality and human sexuality. Gheid Storm is not just male, but a certain kind of male in a specific situation, and Helena is a woman who recognizes her separateness from the kind of sensibility that Storm represents.

At the beginning of the play, Gheid is confident, assertive. He sees Helena as a desirable woman who may be won—it's only a matter of time. His aggressiveness is indicated by his stepping uninvited into her house through the window. When he finds that she is not charmed by his action, he is patronizing, "Well, I like the little insulting women—."[13] His masculine bravado is only one element of his characterization, for he also represents a conventional moral conscience—he has been raised by "upright women." He desires Helena because of what she is, but also condemns what she is. What she represents to him is clear to Helena and the reader, though Storm himself is unaware of his conflict, which is signaled by his name. Specifically, he alludes to her "fine ways," and adds, "though there are many tales of how you came by them." He reports town gossip that "you come through once every Spring, driving a different man ahead of you with a riding whip; another has it, that you come in the night—." Yet he confesses he has come because he needs her, because "I wanted—to know—you," because "of some great ease in your back—the look of a great lover—" (p. 47). His phrases indicate that Helena is an almost mythic object of desire—her name aids this impression.

What attracts him, however, is also what he cannot accept consciously. In spite of alluding several times to her past, he adds that he believes in none of these tales, but in a moment of anger he charges: "You can bury your past as deep as you like, but carrion will out," and finally, "No matter what you've been—done—I love you" (pp. 52, 55). In other words, he will "forgive" her. In Barnes's work "forgiveness" is suspicious activity, for the need to forgive implies the assumed "rightness" of the one who forgives.

Storm's confusion is evident also in his offering Helena "a clean heart" and in his declaration that "He has never gone to the dogs for love" (p. 55). Helena, of course, has. Helena points out the incongruity: "My house is for men who have done their stumbling" (p. 56). She thus refers enigmatically to those who have "fallen," that is, recognized their sensual nature without apology, or repression.

Part of the difficulty of the play resides in its language. Its enigmatic dialogue seems inapplicable to the situation at hand, yet obscurely relevant to an overall pattern. One example is an interchange begun by Gheid's question, "Shall I die, and never have known you?" The tone of the question implies a "you" beyond Helena, a kind of love that she represents, an impression confirmed by his restating his original question: "Shall I have no love like yours?" (p. 57). Her enigmatic response—"Death, for you, will begin where my cradle started rocking—" evokes the idea that her birth is his death. Jungian terms provide a clarification of the idea. Helena can be seen as Gheid's shadow: "the ego's mirror image, composed of unlived or repressed psychic features."[14] Thus, Storm's stepping into Helena's house represents his psychic confrontation. "Conscious realization of the shadow is a step toward wholeness"; this means that for Storm wholeness is a matter of accepting his own sensual nature without also projecting it upon Helena and condemning it. To do so, of course, means "going to the dogs"—to ruin—for love, and consequently a loss of innocence, which means to become conscious of one's motives and desires. In other words, Storm has yet to reach this "death"—this decay, this loss of innocence—which for Helena began long ago. The atmosphere of decay which surrounds Helena symbolically suggests her consciousness.

In this context the exhaustion at the end of the play is appropriate. If the play were about the battle of the sexes, as those who read it as a naturalistic play tend to see it, Helena's exhaustion is confusing. If she had achieved victory, we would expect triumph, not exhaustion. However, the fatigue at the end signals Barnes's refusal to affirm consciousness in glowing terms. Even though Helena possesses an understanding and acceptance of her nature and human nature, the knowledge produces no satisfaction, no triumph. When Storm announces he is leaving, Helena answers, "I cannot touch new things, nor see beginnings." The price of "being herself" is loneliness and alienation. Moral consciousness is a gain, but also a loss. Helena's existence is a melancholy testament to that loss which she embraces but also suffers. But the alternative—Storm's specious assertiveness, his mindless confidence, his innocence—is unnerving. In *To the Dogs*, Barnes has introduced a forceful Gheid Storm whom the audience expects to take control of the situation, but they find Helena possessed of a superior wisdom and assertive in its defense.

The male/female dichotomy in the play exists at the symbolic level where Helena is depicted as possessing ancient wisdom. On this level, Storm's pursuit of Helena is the pursuit of that widsom, or consciousness, which in this work is associated with symbolic death. A similar shade of meaning is conveyed in *Kurzy of the Sea* when Rory hears that his father has brought a mermaid: "Ah, saints save us, it's a real spirit she is, and I'm lost!" Literally he is lost, meaning that he will have to marry; but on a figurative level "lost," implying "destroyed or ruined physically or morally," suggests that his spiritual condition is threatened too: he descends, in fact, to earthly aspirations. The idea recalls the legends of Greek gods who loved mortals and transformed them, usually to a less than human state.

In Barnes's world, one loses spiritual being to descend to earth and mortal life, but like the theological "fortunate fall," this loss "has its fruition." Helena suffers from the burden of human consciousness, and Storm in his uncertain pursuit identifies himself with the spirit of earth and mortality. At this level the play suggests archetypal allegory: earth is the devouting mother, and all of us—male and female—go down to her and to death. In the process we suffer decay, or consciousness of our limited nature. In this sense birth is a loss, a death, but also one that has its "measure of fruition."

The effect of the ambiguous prose here is to force a reader beyond the level of literal meaning. At the surface, the dialogue seems limited to a male/female conflict, though not all details can be interpreted satisfactorily at this level. Unlike *Kurzy* where an audience can successfully remain at the surface level of meaning, *To the Dogs* demands a symbolic reading for a coherent account of its features.

Similar care is required for *Three from the Earth* (November 1919), the first of Barnes's Provincetown productions. As in *To the Dogs*, oblique dialogue and tension between characters pervade this play which takes up sexual repression, a topic demanding some reticence even for Provincetown. The comments of early reviewers indicate that this play puzzled its viewers more than Barnes's later two Provincetown productions— *Kurzy of the Sea* (April 1920) and *An Irish Triangle* (Dec. 1920). Rebecca Drucker wrote: "It floats in a nebula of its own connotations, into which the audience tries to force a baffled entrance." Alexander Woolcott observed that "it is really interesting to see how absorbing and essentially dramatic a play can be without the audience ever knowing what if anything, the author is driving at. . . ."[15] In his 1976 study James B. Scott observed that the play is about Kate's "unnaturalness" in not recognizing her son John.[16] Louis F. Kannenstine concluded that the play "involves the martyrdom of womankind."[17] And biographer Andrew Field has written that "The play's main feature is an ever-promising, never-easing inscrutability."[18]

The ostensible situation of the play is that three brothers have come to Kate Morley to retrieve their father's letters, an act that is soon revealed to be a pretext. In truth, they have come to see if she will acknowledge John as her son. The play's action, therefore, is Kate's discovery of her moral character, or rather the audience's appreciation of her evasion. What the audience experiences is virtually a battle for control: Kate's preservation of her self-esteem or the triumph of the boys in gaining their acknowledgment. The effect of the play is achieved through a series of parallels drawn among three of the characters: Kate, the boys' father, and his wife, even though the latter two never appear on stage. Kate and the father represent repressed natures. Only the mother seems to have accepted her sensual nature.

As the play opens, the boys sit, plainly out of place, in the stylish drawing room. Kate enters, establishing her superiority to them and their life through a series of sharp questions. With rude directness she enquires, "Ah yes, your father—he was a barber, wasn't he," and "Your mother—a prostitute, I believe."[19] To which Henry replies calmly, "At times." Kate becomes cautious when she discovers they know about the letters. She admits she has suffered and also acknowledges her malice, but placates herself with the thought that "We've all been awhile with the dogs, we don't all learn to bark" (p. 19). Her comment reaffirms her sense of superiority. But when she feels threatened again, she turns aggressively against the earthy nature of the mother: ". . . she had an underlip like a balloon—and your father kissed that mouth, was even tempted—" James interrupts, "My father often saw beyond the flesh" (p. 22).

She demeans the boys, charging: "You're ugly, and clumsy, and uncouth. You grunt and roar, you wear abominable clothes—and have no manners—and all because of your father, your mighty righteous and original father. . . . Oh, we all have our pathetic moments of being at our best, but he wasn't satisfied with that, he wanted to be at it all the time. And the result, the life of a mole. 'Listen and say nothing' " (pp. 23–4).

The exchange is puzzling to an audience because Kate's hostility is excessive and seemingly unmotivated by the play's action. However, the reference to the mole provides a clue to Kate's reaction. Barnes may simply have intended the reference to suggest the hidden, repressed life. However, Rémy de Gourmont, mentioned by the boys in the play, discussed the virgin mole in *Natural Philosophy of Love* as an example of an "excessively feminine" flight from the male. A complex symbol, the mole represents not only blindness to life but also fear of sexuality. It is relevant to both the father and Kate. The father's life has consisted of "being at our best," but suddenly he becomes the father of three boys. For her part, Kate exclaims, "Why great God, I might be the mother of one of you!" The comment establishes her belief that they do not know that she indeed is the mother of one of them. However, John's quiet reply, "So I believe, madame," confirms that they do know. Yet Kate acts as if she has not heard him. This refusal is a sign of her repression, for to acknowledge John is to accept her sexuality and perhaps also to accept responsibility for usurping the original mother's place in the family.

The extremity of her attack on the mother and on the father's wavering nature are signs that, like Gheid Storm, she projects onto others traits of her own nature that she refuses to accept. Indeed, Barnes implies Kate's basic similarity with the boys' earthy mother. When Kate recalls the mother, she remembers a pet monkey that has been fed from a pot of honey "kept full by her admirers." Significantly, when Kate questions whether the father had any right to bring "such children as you into the world," Henry adds, "And you also had your pot of honey" (p. 24). The parallel implies the similarity between Kate and the mother rather than a difference which Kate asserts by virtue of her attack.

At the opening of the play, Kate has appeared emotionally self-sufficient. She, it is clear, is not as "delicate" as the father who has retreated from life into sensuality and, unable to come to terms with his own nature, ended by committing suicide. Readers are told that "everything had been too much for him." Kate's facade of superiority breaks finally when the boys, unable to get beyond her recriminations, become angry. Their actions convey the idea that they understand her evasions, even though she refuses to. Henry says in parting: "We won't need to bother you again. We are leaving the country and going elsewhere—and there was only one of us to whom you might have shown a little generosity . . ." (p. 29). When Kate protests their abrupt departure, John takes her in his arms and kisses her on the mouth. "Not that way! Not that way!" Kate cries, but James responds, "That's the way you bore him" (p. 30). Kate's evasion is broken, for a moment, by the incestuous kiss, which is an indictment of Kate's refusal to recognize John and thereby her passionate nature.

The play externalizes Kate's evasion through her confrontation with her son and his two stepbrothers. Once a viewer perceives that the organizing principle of the play is repression, the details of the surface action become coherent, and the play's conclusion, which seems curiously suspended, can be seen as appropriate after all. After the confrontation between the boys and Kate, the air of tension remains. The confrontation does not clear up hostilities; it only exposes the roots of the hostility between them. Thus, the boys' victory inforcing Kate's admission is an empty one: it changes nothing. Kate's "decay," or coming to self awareness, is avoided. But in the tension that lingers and in the boys' intention to go abroad, the play carries a latent criticism of the repressive nature of middle-class American respectability, which the stylish Kate represents, especially in her intended marriage to a "supreme court judge."

Barnes continued the practice of confrontation in *The Dove*, which was included in *A Book* but not produced until 1926. Like *Three from the Earth* and *To the Dogs*, the play is an exploration of desire and repression and an example of Barnes's exploitation of multiple chords to force an audience to rethink expectations. However, the conclusion is complicated by a symbolic gesture and an unexpected, comic end that challenges the audience's views regarding sexuality, specifically lesbianism. One reviewer found *The Dove* a "crisp little essay into abnormality." The reviewer concluded that the play "probably was completely incomprehensible to most of the audience." Another found it a "wearisome talk orgy."[20]

The first scene reveals the air of decadence that Amelia and Vera Burgson attempt, though there is also a humorous, outlandish quality to their devices. Vera confesses:

> . . . we'll never, never be perverse though our entire education has been about knees and garters and pinches on hindquarters—elegantly bestowed—and we keep a few animals—very badly—hoping to see something first-hand—and our beds are as full of yellow pages and French jokes as a bird's nest is full of feathers—God! little one, why do I wear lace at my elbows?[21]

When The Dove, a young woman whom Vera and Amelia have taken into their home, answers that she wears lace because she has pretty arms, Vera responds, "Nonsense! Lace swinging back and forth like that tickling my arms, well, that's not beauty—." To which The Dove replies, "I know." The interchange emphasizes Vera's straining after sensuality— and the falsity of her efforts. Although Vera and Amelia have willingly adopted their calculated sensuality, they are also its victims, though perhaps neither recognizes this. Their room "garish, dealing heavily in reds and pinks," with furniture of "the reclining type" expresses a suppressed inner life that they mask by affecting sensuality.

In response to Vera's feeling of the hopelessness of their lives, The Dove insists that "she has never held anything against hopelessness," implying that the status quo is always volatile for The Dove. In a sense she is innocent of traditional expectations. She scorns "necessary continuity" and wishes "every man were beyond the reach of his own biography" (p. 157). What she resists apparently is the routine acceptance of social pressure, urging the person to develop, to progress, to be something acceptable to the social order, a capitulation that inhibits or warps the self. Amelia and Vera are stunning examples.

As they wait for Amelia's return from shopping, Vera plays with the idea that The Dove is the "mad one" and that she and Amelia are "just eccentric." The Dove sketches her background, as if to certify her own sanity, adding, "I became very fond of moles—it's so daring of them to be in the darkness underground. And then I like the open fields too— they say there's nothing like nature for the simple spirit" (p. 152). Vera adds, "Yes, and I've long had my suspicions of nature." In many of Barnes's early stories, rustic simplicity is suspect; nature is not inherently good. Rather it is inherently and indiscriminately sensual. Still we observe The Dove's remarks both seriously and humorously, recognizing her statement as an oblique allusion to Vera and Amelia, who are leading mole-like lives—daring—in their posing, but in the darkness underground nevertheless. They are as The Dove observes, "Two splendid dams erected about two little puddles" (p. 158). In effect, their passionate pose masks a fear of sexuality.

By the end of the scene the exaggerated sensibilities of Vera and Amelia have been amply demonstrated and further that their sensuality—because it is repressed—estranges them from society. When Vera confesses that she sends Amelia out because she can't let the grocer call for fear he will see the picture of the Venetian courtesans in the hallway, The Dove concludes, "You have cut yourselves off—just because you're lonely" (p. 159). The strained sensibility Barnes presents in Vera and Amelia reaches parody, an inverse parody of propriety, which is presented as sham decadence. Amelia and Vera seem both comic and pathetic.

After Amelia's return, the second scene concludes quickly with Amelia's tirade: "I'd like to tear out all the wires in the house! Destroy all tunnels in the city, leave nothing underground or hidden or useful, oh, God. God!" (p. 162). Kneeling before The Dove, Amelia seeks the sword The Dove has been polishing, but finds instead her hand. The Dove bares Amelia's shoulder and breast and "sets her teeth in." Getting up swiftly, The Dove moves into the foyer, holding a pistol. She calls, "For the house of Burgson," and a shot is heard. Amelia rushes to the hall. She returns with the picture of the two Venetian courtesans with a bullet through it. "*This* is obscene!" she exclaims (p. 163).

Multiple emotional chords are evident in the movement from hysteria to comedy which is created first by Vera's tenseness and then by the absurd exaggerations of Amelia, who finds "disaster everywhere" and illustrates this by telling of a woman who has tried to cheat her out of a quarter at the fish market. Furthermore, the blatant sexuality of the concluding scene gives rise to readers' uncertainty about The Dove's motives. All of these details are calculated to disorient the most observant audience and the most astute reader. Amelia's hysteria just before The Dove leaves the room suggests a tragic conclusion. However, the relief *is*, as Scott observed, decidedly comic when the only casualty is the picture of two courtesans.[22]

Again Barnes has used an unsettling conclusion to force a reconsideration of traditional attitudes. Barnes's *"this"* lingers to tease the audience—precisely, what is obscenity, anyway? The lack of a clear antecedent for *"this"* suggests that Barnes cagily intended to give viewers or readers the opportunity to locate "obscenity" wherever their inclinations led them: in the destroyed picture and what it represents, in The Dove's action, in the action of the play, or in the attitudes the play parodies. In effect, the play suggests that acknowledged sexuality, specifically lesbianism, is to be preferred to repression. This is evident if we examine The Dove's role in the denouement.

Though The Dove's self-assurance is problematical in terms of the audience's expectations, her calm knowing air gains our confidence. We understand early in the first scene that the hysterics of Vera and Amelia are untrustworthy. Nevertheless, the shocking nature of the play's denouement challenges readers' initial confidence in The Dove's character. Part of an audience's uncertainty stems from the character's name. A dove, as a symbol, suggests innocence and purity, even holiness; in Christian symbolism the dove represents the holy spirit. In the play, however, The Dove is allied with sexuality, specifically lesbianism—a difficult form of sexuality for many to accept. The contradiction produces the multiple chords that Barnes had achieved in *Passion Play* with a symbolic setting.

Finally, we must see that The Dove's "For the house of Burgson" is a toast of liberation, the commemoration of a decisive, irrevocable act; her exposing and biting Amelia suggests either "the seal of the spirit upon the flesh," or "the sudden and dangerous action of the instincts upon the psyche."[23] Paradoxically, either interpretation of The Dove's bite implies that the two sisters can no longer affect the pose of experienced courtesans while at the same time denying those instincts. There will be less security, and for this reason Vera's fears of The Dove are justified. The Dove's actions, her "preventing nothing," propel them out of their narrow room, that is, out of their narrow conception of self. The badge of their superiority—the picture of the courtesans—and their alienation has been destroyed. They must create themselves anew. As Scott has concluded, ". . . it is better to live—whatever the manner—than it is to dream about living."[24]

The confrontation between characters that occupies Barnes's drama confirms that she was interested in external action only as it revealed the consciousness of individuals. She dramatized emotional experience by using characters who represented opposed ideas to create echoes among characters or by opposing the values of characters to those of society around them. Specifically, in *The Dove*, Amelia and Vera must acknowledge their sexual nature independent of the expectations of society.

Several years later in the *Theatre Guild* Gorelik feature, she would discuss Gorelik's idea that "crowd theatre" was a first step to achieving the "elastic hour devoted to decay." By then Barnes had already achieved the elastic hour devoted to decay, "which had also its fruition." Her aim was to create the "particular and singular soul" that experiences itself apart from the public. These individuals shape their identity by recognizing their nature rather than by conforming to the expectations of society, thereby ensuring a "richer privacy in the dim future." The aim of living, Barnes implied, is consciousness of self.

3
Necessary Silence

It is important to realize that Barnes's short stories were contemporaneous with the journalism and one-acts and that most of them were published at least a decade before *Nightwood*. Her career as a short fiction writer spanned approximately fifteen years from the appearance of "The Terrible Peacock" in 1914 and "Paprika Johnson" in 1915 to the 1929 issue of *A Night among the Horses*—the same years in which her one-acts and her journalism appeared. Therefore, we can expect the short fiction to demonstrate concerns similar to those that occupied the journalism and the one-acts.

During this period Barnes published approximately thirty stories. Her first collection, *A Book* (1923), contained an assortment of drawings, poems, plays, and short stories. The stories and plays were reissued along with three new stories, the result of her expatriate years, in the 1929 *A Night among the Horses*. In 1962 Barnes revised and edited these stories for the definitive collection of her short fiction, *Spillway*, which is included in *The Selected Works*.

One might argue that Barnes's editing and revisions justify treating the short fiction as part of Barnes's later work. Indeed, the critical commentary of *Spillway* suggests that several critics have approached the *Spillway* collection from the perspective of *Nightwood*. For example, reviewer Kent Cathcart in the Nashville *Tennessean* claimed, "All of her writing has in common a verbal felicity, a comfortless vision, and a feeling of doom. . . ." Barbara Guest of the Washington *Post* observed that ". . . she is a master of the ambivalent, desolate stories of the night world."[1]

Similarly, scholars who have considered the short stories have emphasized the darkness of Barnes's vision in terms that echo the criticism of

Nightwood. For example, Suzanne Ferguson writes of Barnes's characters: "They have abandoned national, racial, and ethical traditions; their human contacts are lacerations. They lack even the integrity in isolation that comforts the characters of Hemingway or the early Faulkner, for they are estranged against themselves."[2] Louis F. Kannenstine argues that the aim of the short stories is to render "the terror of the impossibility of being," and adds that her characters "are finally even estranged from themselves."[3] James B. Scott concludes: "In the deepest sense, her stories can be said to show *how* and *why* death can be the only real affirmation in a meaningless universe."[4] Certainly, such an emphasis is understandable since the stories were reissued in *Selected Works*, along with the novel. However, to read the short stories as an echo of *Nightwood* and its dark vision reduces them unnecessarily to a single bleak theme, overlooking their origin in Barnes's early career and the ways in which her concerns and her expression of them develop. Surely, Ferguson is correct in her estimation that these stories "deserve a wider appreciation, not only as representative work of the modernist period, but as remarkable examples of their genre."[5]

Like the journalism and one-acts of this period, Barnes's short stories show the need for conscious living and art as a way to transcend mortality. Similarly, Barnes's early fiction shares various techniques with with the journalism and the one-acts. In the journalism Barnes had at times articulated double messages, as in the Mizner and Crothers features. And in the one-acts she had exploited "multiple chords" and the contradictory suggestions this implied. In the short fiction, Barnes increasingly exploited indirect presentation and ambiguous meaning, becoming, as she did so, a more consciously modern artist. The difference in her fictional technique is apparent if we compare the uncollected fiction with the stories she chose to collect in *Selected Works*. In the best of the collected fiction Barnes demonstrates an almost enigmatic reticence. She is a presenter of scenes and characters, yet silent as to significance; however, her earliest uncollected fiction reveals very different practices.

Beginnings

A preliminary observation about the kind of fiction Barnes was interested in can be made by comparing her earliest newspaper tales to those she produced three to four years later. Many of the early stories, properly called "tales" by Douglas Messerli, have a complicated plot whose aim is to produce the unexpected twist or concluding surprise. These plots often involve a test or a revelation of character. "The Jest of Jests" (1917) is typical of her early tales. Two men love the Madeleonette. One lover, Josiah, convinces her to test the love of the other man, The Physician, by provoking his jealousy while a pistol loaded with blanks lies within his reach. Simultaneously, The Physician decides to test her courage, as he lacks it himself. He intends to shoot her with a pistol loaded with blanks. When Madeleonette falls at the pistol shot, The Physician thinks she has fainted. Disappointed by her lack of courage, he leaves and sends a note telling of his intention to go to Long Beach to recover from the experience. After The Physician has left, Madeleonette is disgusted at The Physician's actions and puzzled by Josiah's disappearance. She writes The Physician a note relating her disappointment and her plans to go to Long Beach. The notes cross, but The Physician and Madeleonette find each other in Long Beach.

The contrived plot reveals that the final joke is a rather sinister one in which Josiah has plotted Madeleonette's death at the hands of the unsuspecting Physician. As in many of these early stories, the reader is deliberately manipulated by the mechanical plot. Another trait of the early tales is the author's intrusiveness. This story, for example, begins with the author's warning that readers will not understand the circumstances until the story's end; at the end the author concludes: "Thus it comes about that the second paragraph of this story is the last."[6] In this story, by calling attention to her intrusiveness, Barnes seems to be poking fun at the plot of intrigue.

Very quickly Barnes moved away from these practices. Many of the stories published between 1917 and 1923 in the *Telegraph* and *The Little Review* are examples of Barnes's transition from the newspaper tales with their manipulated plots to stories that exploited external events or images to reflect inner conditions. More modern in technique, the transition stories are characterized by authorial restraint; plot is of minor interest. The surprise conclusions of her early stories are replaced by Barnes's growing preference for an ambiguous or an abruptly opaque conclusion.

"The Coward" (August 1917) is a good example of Barnes's transition, of her increasing use of what might be termed symbolic methods. Her concern in this story focuses on "decay," specifically, Varra's recognition of the meaning of her own actions. The plot is simple. Varra has a reputation for courage and is proud of that reputation. Her fiancé Karl declares that he loves her "for her bravery more than anything else." Nevertheless, the reputation also causes Varra some "anxiety"; she feels that she has to continue to prove herself. Suddenly, her fiancé Karl and his friend Monk are arrested for stealing jewels. To save Karl, Varra decides to claim that she stole the jewels. On the first day of the trial she approaches the judge to confess, but faints. However, a day later after Karl has been sentenced, she marches up to the judge and confesses.

Ironically, her confession, which is too late to save Karl, will save Monk whom she hates and who has implicated Karl. The story concludes: "She had forgotten Karl, she had forgotten Monk. She looked at the black curtains with their heavy tassels."[7] The detail seems irrelevant; however, this conclusion implies that Varra has confessed to save her reputation for courage. Two details suggest, moreover, that she recognizes the futility of her attempt to salvage her self-esteem, though others may be deceived by her confession. First, consider her concentration on the dark curtains after she has confessed. On the first day in court Varra associated the curtains with judges, "like something that would finally fall into the cup of life and lie there, black and horrible and menacing, spoiling it at the lips, as mother spoils the beauty of wine, the malignity of vinegar" (p. 140). The curtains, like judges, suggest Varra's conscience that indicts her for her pride. It is not courage that motivates her confession, or even love for Karl, but the need to preserve her self-esteem. Her focus on the curtains in the conclusion, therefore, implies that her self-esteem is not recaptured; she recognizes the deceitfulness of her motive.

The second detail that establishes Varra's recognition of the deceitfulness of her motive is the parallel established between Monk and Varra. Monk has been described as ugly; he is jaunty with a touch of bravado which Varra dislikes "because she sensed in this same bravado her own bravery. . . . The difference lay in this: he was trying to produce an illusion and Varra was trying not to disillusion" (p. 136). By the end of the story Varra realizes that she has confessed to create the illusion of bravery. The key to this realization rests in Varra's recognition that she is ugly. After she has confessed, she looks into a mirror and confirms that she is indeed ugly, ugliness here implying a moral rather than a physical condition. Like Monk after all, she is trying to maintain an illusion. The denouement is implied but complete.

Douglas Messerli, in his reading of this story and others, emphasizes in the introduction to *Smoke and Other Stories* the importance of plot: "Coherent with its thematics of determinism, the structure of most of these tales is almost ploddingly grounded in the logical order of events." He points to the lack of resolution in "The Coward": "Although Varra Kolveed of 'The Coward' proves her courage, the reader has no clear idea of what that means in terms of her life; is she arrested?; how does her confession affect Monk, the man who [sic] she detests?" (p. 14). In focusing on plot and the determinism of Barnes's characters, Messerli passes over Barnes's use of symbolic detail. However, in this story Barnes is doing what Messerli, in the introduction, credits Joyce with, that is, using incidents to serve as symbols of the conditions of his characters: "In Joyce's stories, in short, plot is no longer animus, but is revelation" (p. 15). In fact, the action of "The Coward" is intended to reveal the inner psychology of Varra. She fails to prove her courage, and the symbol of the curtains is a sign of her awareness. The action culminates in Varra's identification with Monk. Whether or not she is arrested is irrelevant to the theme of moral courage.

Stories like "The Coward" and many that Barnes published in the following years demonstrate that she had taken the step to writing modern stories in which "revelation" is primary, action secondary. The cause of this transition from plot-centered fiction to symbolic fiction is a matter of conjecture. Joyce's *Dubliners* had been published in 1914, and Barnes's 1922 interview of Joyce revealed her absorption in Joyce's work between 1914 and 1917:

> I had read *Dubliners* over my coffee during the war, I had been on one or two theatrical committees just long enough to suggest the production of *Exiles,* his one play. The *Portrait* had been consumed, turning from one elbow to the other, but it was not until I came upon his last work that I sensed the singer. . . . Yes, then I realized that Joyce must indeed have begun life as a singer, and a very tender singer, and—because no voice can hold out over the brutalities of life without breaking—he turned to quill and paper, for so he could arrange, in the necessary silence, the abundant inadequacies of life, as a laying out of jewels—jewels with a will to decay.[8]

Barnes's comment reflects her respect for Joyce's work, plus an understanding of its aim: The phrase "for so he could arrange, in the necessary silence, the abundant inadequacies of life" suggests the symbolist interest in arranging images or situations without overt authorial intrusion to state meaning.

Aside from the disappearance of authorial comment from fiction, the modern short story, as Horst Ruthrof points out, has tended to limit its focus, often excluding "enveloping experience in favor of a few items of consciousness." Considerations of space, time, and process are limited to "focus directly on pointed experience."[9] This elimination of everything but the essential situation suggests that the isolation of characters that readers experience in Barnes's fiction is an aspect of her technique rather than a failure of characterization. Varra, for example, is not isolated from her community; in many ways she is typical, the average woman, yet Barnes's singleness of purpose in raising the issue of her moral courage sets Varra apart from daily existence.

In focusing on the motives of a single character, Barnes establishes her area of concern to be the problem of the human race rather than the "social problem of the moment."[10] Her use of the pointed experience and symbols to convey inner states and meaning identify even an early story like "The Coward" as modern. Though "The Coward" was not collected by Barnes, it represents a new direction from the early tales that Barnes referred to as "juvenalia."[11] As a transition work, it is similar in style to the stories of *A Book*, in which the authorial intrusion and mechanical plots of the uncollected tales are replaced by contradiction and reticence. The surprise twist conclusions of the tales are replaced by conclusions that are ambiguous and abrupt—almost flat. Nevertheless, in *A Book* Barnes's themes reveal the familiar antagonism to middle-class complacency and her concern for the individual.

The Mature Fiction

The winnowing process that led to *Spillway* of 1962 establishes what Barnes considered the best of her fiction. In this collection, an edition of the best stories of *A Night among the Horses*, her themes inform structure and character; Barnes exploits indirect statement through the opposition of values, usually represented by two characters. In a 1924 *Dial* review Kenneth Burke had observed the motivating force of Barnes's fiction in her descriptions of her characters: "the descriptions themselves are plots."[12] Increasingly, in these stories, the surface complexity derives from prose that is contradictory and ambiguous, and from abrupt and truncated conclusions. The reader is involved in perceiving, beneath an often contradictory prose surface, latent themes that explore the limitation of material existence and the response of the superior sensibility.

In *Selected Works* Barnes collected only those stories in which themes related to individual integrity and human mortality are most powerful in directing characters and in structuring incident, yet most inconspicuous. Specifically, she deleted many of the stories of *A Book* and *A Night among the Horses* that treated death directly, for example, "No Man's Mare," "Indian Summer," "Mother," and "The Nigger." Despite the omission of many stories treating death from Barnes's definitive collection, her preoccupation with death is still apparent. Nevertheless, in the stories that remain death is part of the framework of life. Barnes does not focus on the nature of death—its deceit, or unfairness, or its release. Instead, death is a fact that motivates the need for conscious living rather than evasion. Its presence is the essential condition of human existence. Against this fact human beings in Barnes's fictional world shape their passage.

The following three stories are representative of the best of Barnes's mature fiction. In "A Night among the Horses," "The Rabbit," and "The Valet," Barnes reflects a materialistic view of reality but emphasizes also the value of consciousness. "A Night among the Horses" (December

1918) relates John's struggle to "know what he is." The issue is the effect of materialistic values on the human spirit, a theme that has occupied Barnes in the journalistic features and in many of the one-acts. This story is usually interpreted as a contest between John and Freda, whose destructive social world contrasts with the harmony of John's natural world.

However, the imagery demonstrates that both worlds are hostile. Tangled vines and images of oblivion dominate the natural world. At one point John, peering through "thickly tangled branches," sees "standing against the darkness, a grove of white birch shimmering like teeth in a skull."[13] Similarly, the world of the horses is threatening, not idyllic; "The soft menacing sound deepened as heat deepens; the horses, head-on, roared by him, their legs rising and falling like savage needles taking purposeless stitches" (p. 30). The horses are also described as "galloping about as though in their own ball-room," blurring further the distinction between the social and the animal world: the indoor ballroom and that of the horses.

Another passage illustrates the separation between man and nature: "A frog puffed forth its croaking unmemoried cry; the man struggled for breath, the air was heavy and hot, as though he were nested in a pit of astonishment" (p. 29). Abstract and concrete, the phrase "nested in the pit of astonishment" suggests a birth image, or metaphorically, man's consciousness of his separation from nature. There is ease in the frog's cry, which contrasts with the man's struggle to breathe. Thus, the subject of the story, established implicitly through symbols and parallel themes, is man's desire to make a mark—not to be "unmemoried."

Freda seems to offer this opportunity. She proposes to step John "up from being a 'thing,'" to make him a gentleman. Like Addie of "The Rabbit," Freda is doll-like and mechanical: "that small fiery woman with a battery for a heart and the body of a toy, who ran everything, who purred, saturated with impudence, with a mechanical buzz that ticked away her humanity" (p. 31). Her description identifies her not only with material reality but also with the horse/animal imagery that pervades the story. She is described as "a little beast," "a preying mantis," and like a horse, "She almost whinnied as she circled on her heels."

John greets her proposal at first with comic indignation: "He blew down his mustache. Freda, with that aggravating floating yellow veil! He told her it was 'aggravating,' he told her that it was 'shameless,' and stood for nothing but temptation. He puffed out his cheeks, blowing at her as she passed" (p. 31). Indeed, the yellow veil is a temptation; moreover, John's desire to be something other than an ostler is what has given Freda the control over him that she possess. He tells her, "I *could* stop you, all over, if I wanted to." *If he wanted to* suggests he is willing to enter the world she offers. His characterization of her confirms his ambition and the source of it:

> The kind of woman who can't tell the truth; truth ran out and away from her as though her veins were pipettes stuck in by the devil; and drinking, he swelled, and pride had him, it floated him off.

The language suggests a kind of "fall," for the "he" referred to is certainly not the devil; it is John, and his pride makes him vulnerable to Freda. In the final scene of the story John has just left the party after drawing a circle on the floor around Freda, as if to break his enchantment. Having crawled through the underbrush to the field where the horses are kept, he moves into the field, thinking to take one of them and escape. When they sweep past him, he is horrified, and hollers, "Bitch," blaming Freda for making him a thing they fail to recognize. Though he seems to have rejected his desire to be something by rejecting Freda, his final lines confirm his ambition. Lying in the field, he sobs, "I can do it, damn everything, I can get on with it; I can make my mark!" The horses trample him as they again circle the field. With the abrupt conclusion Barnes suggests the impossibility of returning to a state of innocence. John can no longer be a simple ostler. His fear of what he will be after Freda is through with him is justified.

By pointing, in the title, "A Night among the Horses," to the ballroom imagery associated with the social and natural worlds, Barnes draws together the ballroom and the field, signifying the spiritual darkness that pervades both. They are not opposites: they are one. Both worlds are deceptive, both destructive. While Barnes appears to exploit a context between John and Freda, she in fact questions the basic human motivation to make a mark, to achieve something. That effort appears futile in the world of nature, which is hostile or at best indifferent to man and in which human consciousness perceives man as apart from nature—yet equally futile is the material and limited social world of Freda Buckler. Barnes exposes a false dilemma in this story, for life is not a choice between pastoral simplicity and social values, including progress and ambition. Rather the abrupt ending implies that mortality itself is the limiting factor of life.

Another early story, "The Rabbit," published in October of 1917, is similar in many ways to "A Night," though this story focuses more directly on Rugo's decay: his coming to conscious realization of his situation. However, critics generally conclude that Rugo's experience represents a personal loss for him, partly because of the ambiguous conclusion. Ferguson, Kannenstine, and Scott agree that though Addie has won him, he is destroyed. However, the conclusion—whether Addie has won Rugo—is predictably uncertain, and perhaps irrelevant, for while the plot line develops the story of Rugo's love for Addie, the imagery suggests also Rugo's birth of consciousness, a birth that is both a gain and a loss—decay has its "measure of fruition." Barnes's ambiguous conclusion avoids a typical denouement, insisting on complexity, the lack of resolution inherent in reality.

Rugo's "expulsion" from an Edenic pastoral world occurs almost without his awareness of it. At the beginning of the story Hugo lives in the country, peacefully happy with his animals and farm work. His misfortune arrives in the shape of an inheritance that his people urge him to take, for it "might 'educate' him, make him into an 'executive,' a 'boss,' a man of the world." He acquiesces, almost unconsciously, neither affirming nor resisting, though his rural life has been a constant source of pleasure: "The world lived here and moved, and its incidental placing of him where he could profit by it was the thing that amazed and satisfied him."[14] Once in the city, however, he visualizes himself "sewing, up on a table, as though he had died and had to work it out" (p. 45). Metaphorically, his work is punishment, suggesting the biblical parallel of Adam's fall and expulsion from Eden.

Rugo is attracted to a small Italian girl whose willingness to degrade him seems her primary trait. Addie is described as a "sly baggage" and "neither as nice as he thought, nor as young"; she has a "crouching tongue." Rugo confuses this girl with all of the madonnas he has seen on calendars. Thus, he is hurt by her charges that he is nothing, and he is determined in his simple-minded way to prove his worth. He does so by taking a live rabbit from the butcher across the street and strangling it.

What in paraphrase invites a smile of incredulity from the reader and in the course of the narration a short-lived guffaw from Addie is portrayed effectively in Barnes's prose as a trauma for Rugo: "The terrible, the really terrible thing, the creature did not squeal, wail, cry: it panted, as if the wind were blunt; it thrashed its life, the frightful scruffling of the overwhelmed, in the last trifling enormity" (p. 52).

Before he settled on the rabbit, nearly in a mood of distraction and desperation, Rugo had looked again at Addie, and this time she did not remind him of a calendar madonna:

> He looked at her in sorrow. The cruel passing twist of the mouth— (everything about her was fleeting), the perishing thin arms, the small cage of the ribs, the too long hair, the hands turning on the wrists, the sliding narrow feet, and the faint mournful sharp odour of lemons that puffed from her swinging skirt, moved him away from her; grief in all his being snuffed him out. (P. 49)

Rugo no longer sees Addie as he once had; he has lost an innocence of perception. Rugo's killing the rabbit is a symbolic gesture, his acknowledgment of a difference within—no longer done to win Addie, for he tells her to "take it or leave it." The act signals the death of a part of Rugo, but also a birth—the thrashing quality evoked applies equally well to death and birth—referring here specifically to Rugo's growing awareness of Addie's character. After he has killed the rabbit, Addie becomes fearful, for he seems different. She asks, as he leaves the room, "Where are you going?" The story concludes: "He did not seem to know where he was, he had forgotten her. He was shaking, his head straight up, his heart wringing wet" (p. 53).

Barnes gives the reader little to draw on in terms of the identity of the new Rugo. There is the lingering irony of the advice of Rugo's people, who have hoped he would become "a man of the world." Perhaps he has, but the price has been a trusting quality and gentleness of character. Yet there is value in seeing the Addies of the world clearly, though the world also may seem impoverished as a result. What is certain is that Rugo at the end of the story is not the same man who "let Armenia slip through his fingers" (p. 44). For Rugo consciousness is not achieved without the loss of illusions. Whether the change in Rugo is good or bad is likely to be the wrong question. It is both. Barnes refuses to reinforce either implication, for she seems interested primarily in creating the metaphor of coming to consciousness with its attendant struggle.

In both "A Night among the Horses" and "The Rabbit" Barnes portrays a materialistic world. In "A Night" both social and natural worlds seem equally destructive. In "The Rabbit" a natural Edenic world is lost, and Rugo is condemned to a social world that is destructive, though its final effect on Rugo is ambiguous: his experience represents both a loss and a gain. In "The Valet" Barnes examines human limitations against the background of nature, which is identified with fruitfulness but also with death. However, through the character of the valet, Vanka, Barnes symbolizes the artist's work, which transcends the natural world and may achieve lasting value.

"The Valet" (May 1919), which Kannenstine reads as a story of suppressed passion, depends almost entirely on contradictory suggestions and a shift of focus, via the title, to Vanka.[15] Though the title asserts the importance of Vanka, the valet, the narrative traces the decline of Louis-Georges whose character is subtly criticized. He makes a show of knowing: he pretends to know about his racing stock but unwittingly reveals a hearty, friendly ignorance. He farms but knows little about it; he plans but his "fierce pride," coupled with lack of knowledge and execution, suggests that he follows rather than orders nature. His death is presented as part of the order of nature. It is slow, described as a "founder-ing" or ripening: "Louis-Georges ripened into death" (p. 40).

Further criticism of his character is the result of what appear to be extraneous characters in the story. There are two women who are sisters; one has a child and a nagging sense of guilt: "In her youth Leah had evidently done something for which she now prayed at intervals, usu-ally before a wooden Christ hanging from a beam in the barn. . . ." (p. 38). Barnes refers to the subject a second time after the death of Louis-Georges when Vanka observes:

> Of course Leah had made a scene, hardly to be wondered at, considering. She had brought her baby in, dropping him beside the body, giving her first order: "You can play together, now, for a min-ute."
> Vanka had not interfered. The child had been too frightened to disturb the arranged excellence of Louis-Georges' leavetaking, and both the child and the mother soon left the room in stolid calm. (P. 42)

The scene and its reporting are curious. Why is it "hardly to be wondered at"? Is the reader to understand that the child may have been Louis-Georges's or merely that Louis-Georges has taken in Leah and her child? One situation works to the credit of Louis-George, the other does not. The passages, and Louis-Georges's relationship to Vera Sovna, whom the neighbors believe to be "something" to Louis-Georges, seem intended to raise questions about Louis-Georges's character, questions that are unresolved.

The conclusion of the story is characteristically enigmatic. After Louis-Georges's death, Vanka prepares the body and returns to his room, feeling that he "had left something undone. . . . He loved service and order; he loved Louis-George who had made service necessary and order desirable" (p. 42). Vanka's feeling of uneasiness is interrupted when Vera Sovna climbs the vine to his window. She enters the room, exclaiming, "Most fortunate man, most elected Vanka! He let you touch him, close, close, near the skin, near the heart. . . . You knew him, all of him, for years. Tell me—tell me, what was he like?" (p. 43).

Recovering from his astonishment at the intensity and the nature of her outburst, Vanka calms her: "I will tell you, if you are still, if you will sit down, if you are quiet," and then he continues, "His arms were too long, but you know that, you could see that, but beautiful; and his back, his spine, tapering, slender, full of breeding—" (p. 43). Figuratively, Vanka assumes, with his telling, the role of artist, creating from the physical traits of Louis-George the character of the aristocratic gen-tleman.

The word *breeding*, though, disrupts our participation in Vanka's recreation, for we recall Louis-Georges's bluff ribaldry, praising the "breeding" of his racing stock: "There's more breeding in the rump of one of these, than any butt in the stalls of Westminister" (p. 37). The quiet irony of "breeding" and its related uses—one opening, the other closing the story—plus the subtle rumors concerning the character of Louis-Georges, alert us to Vanka's efforts. Vanka, as artist, interprets and transforms external reality into something timeless. The loss both Vanka and Vera experience is transformed by Vanka's creation of order: art is the channel in this story whereby excessive emotion is released, creating an image of Louis-Georges which is superior to the Louis-Georges who has "ripened into death." The image of Louis-Georges that Vanka creates is partially a deception, of course. However, the deception achieves its own triumph over mutability, and thereby its truth. In memorializing, art defeats time as life cannot; art, therefore, though a lie, is also a superior reality—a concept common to symbolist thought.

All three of these early stories (1917–19), "A Night among the Horses," "The Rabbit," and "The Valet," demonstrate naturalistic conceptions of the external world. The social and natural worlds are important backgrounds against which characters define themselves, but the use of natural or social backgrounds does not make these stories naturalistic. In *The Symbolist Movement* Balakian describes a significant difference between naturalist and symbolist concerns. Naturalists, she points out, concern themselves with social and hereditary forces, but symbolists are "concerned with man's mental reactions to and reconciliations with the natural order of the cosmos. . . ."[16] What distinguishes Barnes's stories from the naturalistic tradition, then, is her emphasis on the process by which inner, perhaps unconscious feelings come into an individual's consciousness. Barnes focuses on the birth of the individual's consciousness of the human condition, including death, and the reactions of a character to this awareness. Her concern is with man's sense of his place in the flow of time. In "A Night among the Horses," John wavers between acceptance and rejection of Freda's world, which is the social world: he enters that world or faces the oblivion of the natural world. In "The Rabbit" Rugo's loss of innocence touches the mythic theme of expulsion, with the ambiguous gain of the knowledge of good and evil and death. In "The Valet," art is seen as something that triumphs over the oblivion of nature.

These stories, representative of Barnes's maturing style, present the problem of coming to consciousness and the price of consciousness in losing a stable, predictable system of life and values. All three indicate Barnes's interest in the human response to the human condition. In none of them does she invoke the sentimental desire for a return to a settled world; she does not look back with nostalgia. Her emphasis is on conscious realization of the nature of the human condition and an awareness of mortality. Her characters enact their separation from nature and from middle-class society.

By creating distance between readers and characters through contradictory or ambiguous actions and through difficult and ambiguous prose, Barnes prohibits a reader's emotional identification with characters, demanding instead the distance of an observor. As a result, readers discern the idea beneath the experience of Barnes's characters. Barnes perfects these techniques in the following group of stories in which the structuring idea has all but disappeared beneath details that are exquisitely arranged in prose that conceals as it reveals.

Fruition

All of the following stories are the result of Barnes's Paris years, with the exception of "Spillway," which appeared in December 1919 as "Beyond the End." Like the magazine journalism and plays, these stories focus on women. "Aller et Retour," "Spillway," "Cassation," "The Grande Malade," and "The Passion" offer more complexity than the stories previously discussed. This is true because so *little* seems to happen; indeterminate language and pointed experience create double meanings. Barnes's aim in these stories is to reveal the qualities that motivate her fictional heroines. Though the main characters in the previous group had often seemed victims, the main characters in the stories that follow are, as Scott noted, "fighters." Even though Scott emphasizes the determinism of Barnes's characters, his evaluation that "the best of them" maintain "an amazing fidelity to their own lights" is an intriguing insight, for it hints at something other than determinism in the makeup of Barnes's characters.[17] At the center of each story is a limited number of characters, usually two. These characters do not change. What happens is that the reader gains an insight through their interaction.

In "Aller et Retour" Barnes arranges symbols, patterns, and actions to establish the strength of Madame von Bartmann, but she also develops, in counterpoint, the character's limitations. At issue is the limited, fatalistic vision of Madame von Bartmann. James B. Scott, for example, treats this work as a naturalistic and autobiographical statement by Barnes. Scott argues: "Madame's tragic vision of life's repetitious uselessness is an extension of the author's."[18] However, Ferguson, author of the only study devoted solely to the short fiction, detects weakness in Madame von Bartmann; Ferguson concludes that "for all her knowledge," she is "not a person either."[19] Kannestine's view is that

Madame von Bartmann is a positive figure. Questioning Ferguson's claim that Madame von Bartmann is limited, he argues that she is "one of Miss Barnes's women who have come to some terms with the mortal agony."[20]

Barnes's technique in this story is to present Madame as she returns home and then to record her effect on her daughter, Richter. Resolution of the situation depends on readers' perception of nuances and apparently irrelevant details and on their adoption of Richter's perspective in order to feel the contradiction between Madame's ideas and actions and to appreciate their implications. In truth, "Aller et Retour" is a criticism of Madame von Bartmann, who returns after her husband's death and after years of absence to see what he has made of their daughter, Richter.

We are told in an opening one-sentence paragraph that Madame Von Bartmann is a "woman of great strength" (p. 3). We anticipate seeing that strength in action so that it may be defined more precisely. While she waits in Marseilles for her train to depart, Madame passes through the streets, observing. She seems able to accept everything that she sees along the littered streets: a woman, surrounded by young women, plucks the feathers from a robin; windows are filled with cheap funeral wreaths and religious symbols; she goes to church and prays for a "common redemption," but is more interested in the quality of the altar cloth and the absence of burning candles.

A single motif, woven through the story like a background chord, suggests indirectly that thinking is not Madame's strength. She washes her hands in the hotel, "trying to think." She puts down *Madame Bovary,* having "read a few sentences with difficulty." She prays "with all her vigorous understanding." As she sits talking to Richter, her posture mimics Rodin's *The Thinker:* "She leaned forward, her elbow on her knee, her face in her palm" (p. 8).

What seems to be her strength is her understanding of life and her expectations of Richter. Her view of life rushes forth in a torrent of epigrams and contradictory assertions: She claims that one must achieve a "great understanding, or accomplish a fall," but also that "Contemplation leads to prejudice. . . . Man is rotten from the start. . . . Rotten with virtue and with vice. He is strangled by the two and made nothing; and God is the light the mortal insect kindled, to turn to, and to die by. . . . and don't misconstrue the value of your passions; it is only seasoning to the whole horror." She breaks off in tears and asks if Richter is thinking. When she answers, "no," Madame urges, "Think everything, good, bad, indifferent; everything, and *do* everything, *everything!* Try to know what you are before you die." Then, a touch melodramatically, she says, "putting her head back and swallowing with shut eyes, 'come back to me a good woman' " (pp. 9–10).

If, as Scott and Kannenstine argue, Madame von Bartmann's strength is her vision of life, her weakness has to be her inability to act in accordance with that view. When Richter timidly approaches her mother several days later, "shy, frightened, and offended," and asks permission to announce her engagement to Mr. Teal, readers are dismayed by Madame's unexpected approval, especially after her impassioned talk about Richter going out and doing everything, about "finding out what you are before you die." One suspects that Madame von Bartmann acquiesces because she can see no alternative. Her wisdom of life is that it is suffering. She does not "possess the great understanding" which might liberate Richter, only a fatalistic sense of necessity that dooms Richter to repeat her own life.

Thus, the concluding line, Madame's "Ah, how unnecessary" is indeed ambiguous. Certainly critics have interpreted it in various ways. Scott suggests that Madame's remark comments on the futility of the cycle of marriage, birth, and death, which Richter enters by marriage.[21] Ferguson reads the phrase as Madame's judgment on the staid life that opens before Richter. More important, Ferguson discerns that Madame's failure to do better for Richter is a mark of her own superficiality. But Ferguson also sees Richter as superficial in desiring the marriage.[22] However, Richter's desire for the marriage is not clearly established. She reports only what her father has arranged, and she displays no pleasure when her mother agrees to the marriage: she sat quietly at the table and "did not look up" (p. 11). One can understand certainly that Richter feels betrayed and sentenced to the kind of fate her mother has fled. Richter's experience, whatever it is, will be *unnecessary*. Its futile circularity will occur partially because Madame von Bartmann is incapable of seeing life in any other way than as suffering.

An interesting detail of the story, which subtly points to her weakness, is the association of insects—mentioned three times—with Madame von Bartmann.[23] In his "Translator Postscript" to Rémy de Gourmont's *The Natural Philosophy of Love*, Pound differentiates species "according to their apparent chief desire, or source of choosing their species":

> Insect, utility; bird, flight; mammal, muscular splendour; man, experiment.
> The insect representing the female, and utility; the need of heat being present, the insect chooses to solve the problem by hibernation, i.e., a sort of negation of action.[24]

The principle "negation of action" characterizes Madame von Bartmann exactly. Her inability to act on another vision of life betrays Richter to the circularity that Madame laments in her final comment, "Ah, how unnecessary." Madame's coming and going have been unnecessary, for she has accomplished nothing. In "Aller et Retour," through negation of action, the mother as victim is perpetuated in Richter because of Madame's limited vision. Metaphorically, Madame and Richter represent poles of a drama in which the spirit (child) is betrayed by confining materialism and fatalism.

In contrast to Madame von Bartmann's giving in to the inevitable is the courage of Julie in "Spillway." Originally published in December 1919 as "Beyond the End," "Spillway" is one of Barnes's best short stories. One of the difficulties of this story is that initially readers are not likely to identify with Julie. Her responses to the old man, who drives her home from the sanitarium where she has been for five years, and to her daughter Ann are abrupt, and her anger is apparent—"fixing her angry eyes straight ahead" (p. 62)—though its source is not so clear. She responds irritably to Pater, who is pleased to see her, "You're looking splendid, Julie." He is concerned about her health: "It's a drop here of fifteen hundred feet—but your heart—that is good—it always was" (p. 64). Julie responds to this solicitude with anger: "What do you know about my heart? You don't know what you are talking about." In response, readers are inclined to be sympathetic to Paytor.

In addition to this harshness of character, Julie's apparent longing for moral certainty encourages readers to see traditional values as positive: "If only I had the power to feel what I should feel . . ." (p. 69). The central question in terms of Julie's character, however, is whether readers are to see her lack of conventional values as positive or negative. In fact, her homecoming is a symbolic testing of conventional values, represented by Paytor, and these values are seen to be lacking. They have not been able to sustain Julie nor are they able to uphold Paytor.

While Julie has been at a tuberculosis sanitarium, she has had a child by a patient who has since died. She returns home with mixed emotions to face her husband Paytor, who has never been told about the child because Julie expected that she and the child (also afflicted) would die and Paytor would never know of her infidelity.

Because of her illness, she has lost a traditional system of beliefs and developed values that she distrusts because they are alien to traditional values. In order to test her values she returns to Paytor, who represents the touchstone of conventional morality. "Division," therefore, is a feeling that Julie desires, for that would make her wrong. She would feel guilt and in doing so participate in conventional moral codes. At least then she would experience moral sureness.

Julie's present values have grown from her consciousness of death. She explains to Paytor: "But think of this: me a danger to everyone—excepting those like myself—in the same sickness, and expecting to die. . . ." (p. 65). She recognizes her fear: ". . . and nothing coming after, no matter what you do, nothing at all, nothing at all but death . . ." (p. 66). She longs for a "design," that is, a reason, for the torment she and, by implication, humanity alike face, but she sees none. She clings to life because that is all she sees, and life, symbolically, takes the form of perpetuating life—thus her affair and her daughter Ann.

She tells Paytor of her mixed emotions, both shame and "a sort of hysterical joy." She hopes that Paytor will understand, while she admits also that he lacks this "grace," which she defines as "perception, that strange other 'something,' that must be at the center of everything (or there wouldn't be such a sensuous desire for it). . . ." Her fears, however, are correct, for Paytor responds by asking if she doesn't feel horror, "in a loud voice," which indicates both his anger and disorientation. Paytor, who walks with a "dependable gait," clings to rigidly delineated standards and ideas. When she tells him about the child, he ". . . turned away from her" (p. 66). He is unable to cope with the complexity that Julie's life symbolizes and which her return brings.

Because of readers' initial uncertainty regarding Julie's character, they may be inclined to blame Julie for her infidelity and for her departure from traditional moral codes, as Paytor does. But Barnes has frequently included readers within a moral community which she then attacks through humor or abandons. She does this here with great subtlety, for by associating Paytor—his name means *father*—with rigid codes, religious values, and with death, Barnes abandons him as the moral center of the story. This is achieved through Julie's memory of a childhood incident while she sits in the darkened living room, listening to Paytor's pacing in the attic. Julie remembers "the day they had made her kiss the cheek of their dead priest [father] . . . that had made her cry with a strange backward grief that was swallowed, because in touching his cheek she kissed aggressive passivity, entire and cold" (pp. 68–69). By contrast Julie's energy is directed toward life: her giving birth to Ann and even her uncertainty reveal the desire for life that animates her. The desire for design—"a thing should make a design; torment should have some meaning" (p. 66)—marks her as an emblem of the artist.

While Julie has discarded old conventions, she lacks, so far, confidence in the feelings that replace them. But her uncertainty is her strength. By contrast, Paytor's certainty is his weakness. Appalled by Julie's confession, he is unable to feel any sympathy or pity for her or for the child. His first consideration is her betrayal of him and the values by which he rules his life. With those certainties denied, he can no longer live.

The denouement of the story, like the narration itself, draws on suggestion. In trying to think of the "right word before it happens," Julie kneels to the floor:

> "But if I put my head down, way down—down, down, down . . ."
> She heard a shot. "He has quick warm blood—"
> Her forehead had not quite touched the boards, now it touched them, but she got up immediately, stumbling over her dress. (P. 70)

Julie is confronted once more with death, this time, presumably, Paytor's, though his death is suggested, never confirmed. Given the strength Julie has demonstrated previously, readers are not likely to doubt her ability to continue. Paytor's death is yet another "stumbling over her dress," that is, fragile, physical nature. All in all, Julie's strength of spirit is admirable. To see her too realistically, however, invites us to see her as responsible for Paytor's death, which she is not. She, like many of Barnes's characters, is emblematic, a representation of an idea. Her acceptance of uncertainty is positive; her sensibility reflects an awareness of the complexity of life and the destructiveness of simplistic attitudes.

The abrupt conclusion—one might more accurately call it an abrupt inconclusiveness—of this story, as in many of Barnes's later stories, seems intended to raise issues, to break simple patterns of response. The uncertainty of human values and the complexity of life faced by those aware of its multiple claims resist simplistic resolution. Julie perceives the complexity of the world, yet faces it, acting out of her responses. She accepts, as does Madame von Bartmann, but she also faces life with courage, not just resignation. In her acceptance of the validity of her own response to the external world, Julie achieves moral integrity. In doing so, she anticipates the superior sensibility, the artist.

The nature of the artist and her relationship to the external world is the subject of "Cassation," "The Grande Malade," and "The Passion." In "Cassation" Barnes presents not a judgment on detachment and innocence or suffering and madness, but a symbolic representation of the human condition that gives rise to both. "Cassation" and "The Grande Malade," in which Katya is a central character, appeared originally in 1925. "Cassation," originally titled "A Little Girl Tells a Story to a Lady," was a new story added to those selected from *A Book* to make up the 1929 volume of *A Night among the Horses.* "The Grande Malade," originally published in *This Quarter* I, and titled, "The Little Girl Continues," was not collected until the 1962 edition of *Spillway.* Both works, told from the point of view of a young girl speaking to an older lady, focus on the nature of reality and the individual's accommodation to it. The control-

ling symbol of "Cassation" is Gaya's daughter, the idiot child Valentine.
The young narrator, Katya, describes her:

> It was beautiful in the corrupt way of idiot children; a sacred beast
> without a taker, tainted with innocence and waste time; honey-haired
> and failing, like those dwarf angels on holy prints and valentines, if
> you understand me, Madame, something saved for a special day that
> would not arrive, not for life at all. . . . (P. 17)

The child is physical being, unconscious of being—as Gaya describes
it: vacancy, incapable of moral action, though the form of the innocence
is pointless. The child symbolizes also the mystery of all being, physical
existence with no apparent purpose. She is the natural world, uncaring
and uncomprehending.

In their relation to the child, Gaya and Katya represent the extremes of
human response. Gaya is one of Barnes's troubled women with a weak
boy-like husband. Like Madame von Bartmann in "Aller et Retour," Gaya
owns a battlefield picture that hangs over the bed. The motif suggests
that fatalistic outlook which sees life as a constant struggle, destined to
be lost.

When Katya meets Gaya, she gives up her ambition to be a dancer,
goes to live with Gaya, and becomes "a religieuse." She is treated like a
child with overtones of a lover. Katya describes the relationship: "I loved
her very much because there was nothing between us but this strange
preparation for sleep," a preparation that mirrors in part the role Gaya
has devised for Katya as companion to her child Valentine (p. 16).

In a wild speech addressing Valentine, Gaya proposes that Katya will
stay with Valentine in the room always:

> Katya will go with you [out to the garden]. She will instruct you, she
> will tell you there are no swans, no flowers, no beasts, no boys—
> *nothing*, nothing at all, just as you like it. No mind, no thought,
> nothing whatsoever else. No bells will ring, no people will talk, no
> birds will fly, no boys will move, there'll be no birth and no death; no
> sorrow, no laughing, no kissing, no crying, no terror, no joy; no
> eating, no drinking, no games, no dancing; no father, no mother, no
> sisters, no brothers—only you, only you! (P. 19)

Gaya, burdened by too much thought, eventually ends in denial of all
meaning, all reality, asserting only the existence of a perceiving "I,"
which, lacking external reality, is only *vacancy.* The philosophical problem, of course, is that she cannot accept lack of purpose and meaninglessness without a bitter sense of betrayal and loss. Therefore, in her

identification with Valentine, Gaya reverts to a less human level, denying consciousness and individuality. As the title of the story indicates,
Gaya breaks, or annuls, the terms of human life. Gaya identifies completely with that aspect of self which represents physical being, metaphorically rejecting both consciousness and external reality. Her love is
self-consuming, turned in upon itself. In her inability to separate her
identity from the daughter as physical being, the self, Gaya rejects as she
turns inward, Katya, the surrogate daughter who represents both individuality and perception of external reality. Katya, however, moves
beyond her withdrawal, which has begun in spring, and ends also a year
later in the spring. She moves once again into the external world.

Katya emerges from her year as "a religieuse" making no judgments,
simply reporting her experience. Katya, who refuses to deny everything
to become Valentine's companion, is preserved by her acceptance of
meaninglessness; in effect she separates the ego from the extremity of
suffering that destroys Gaya. She is restless, a seeker. On a realistic level,
the events have a nightmare quality that is particularly troubling in view
of the noncommittal quality of Katya's narration. Troubling events are
reported flatly and without emotion, as if they are commonplace. The
"innocent ingenuousness" of Katya invites condemnation, as she seems
to float through the world unaffected by misfortune. Yet however unnerving, Katya's retelling of the story to an unidentified "Madame"
attests to its importance for her. Her "confession" to a nameless
"Madame" is in itself an effort of contact, a move not to separation but to
understanding. Katya represents articulation as an implement of control,
or at least acceptance. As narrator of the story, she suggests the artist.
Seen from Katya's perspective, the alternatives are despair because of
human limitation or an escape into art and artifice where external reality
may be transcended; suffering may become art. And one's passion may
again be life and love. One has, after all, to live. This theme is continued
in "The Grande Malade," a companion to "Cassation." Again, Katya and
the listening Madame supply the form of the narrative.

"The Grande Malade" is singularly translucent—that is, the action is
clear, but the meaning remains elusive.

Critics who comment on the story generally agree that it is about the
superficiality of two sisters, Katya and Moydia, and the meaningless,
empty lives they lead. Scott writes that the sisters "are caught in the
superficial ways of the sophisticate."[25] His view is similar to that of
Kannenstine who sees Moydia as "estranged from life and from her own
emotions." She is "Lydia Steptoe . . . seeing herself clearly, perhaps for
the first time, in a mirror."[26] In his reading, the story is also a parody of
café society, recalling the figures of Raymond Radiquet and Jean Coc-

teau. Ferguson comments that the Russian sisters "move on," typical of the characters in Barnes's stories that "explore estrangement and terror of life without love. . . ."[27]

However, readers who condemn the superficiality of Katya and Moydia overlook the values of the decadent tradition and Barnes's early relation to it and neglect important differences between the two sisters. In an early feature for *Bruno's Weekly*, Barnes had shown a humorous approval of decadent values:

> How much do we owe to those of us who can flutter and find decorative joy in fluttering away this small alloted hour. . . .
> The public—or in other words that part of ourselves that we are ashamed of—always turns up the lip when a dilettante is mentioned, all in a patriotic attempt to remain faithful to that little home in the fifties with its wax flowers, it narrow rockers and its localisms, and above all, to that mother whose advice was always as correct as it was harmful.

The dilettante, she continued, "is always about to pass through that incomparable hour, the hour before and the hour after the supper that may prove the last. And so it is that he . . . has discovered that little something that makes the difference between him and the you, who have ordered supplies home for the week."[28] Barnes's comment suggests her approval of the cultivation of sensibility at the expense of prudential wisdom that sacrifices pleasure and beauty for material needs.

Thus, the extravagence and artificiality of Katya and Moydia, which is consistent with the decadent tradition, is a rebellion against meaningless and mundane reality. Only the superior soul had the sensitivity and imagination to live beautifully. Nevertheless, as she had done in her earlier journalism, Barnes allows readers also to smile at the spirited exaggerations of the two sisters.

Katya reveals to the unknown listener that Moydia's ambition is to "become '*traqique*' and '*triste*' and '*tremendous*' all at once, like the great period Frenchwomen, only fiercer and perhaps less *pure*, and yet to die and give up the heart like a virgin." Katya observes, "It was a noble, an impossible ambition, *n'est-ce pas*, Madame?" (p. 21). In taking a lover, Moydia signals her participation in life; she says on learning of his death, "Now I have a great life!" (p. 28). And she is faithful to the pose of the forlorn lover; she wears the cape "until something yet more austere drives the cape away" (p. 22). In dedicating herself to life, Moydia also embraces death: her lover is "beastly with *finis*." He is *"belle-d'un-jour,"* literally, a flower similar to the morning glory, symbolizing the transitoriness of life and perhaps reputation.

In a study of the French poetic tradition, Wallace Fowlie points out an aspect of Baudelaire's aesthetic that is relevant to Katya and Moydia's rootlessness. Fowlie refers to the tradition of the "voyou," the restless adventurer, poet, clown, who is a seeker involved in "quest for what is unseizable, unreal, absurd."[29] Fowlie further describes the voyou:

> The voyou and his brother the clown teach us that true fantasy does not exist and that joy in its purest state is not human. All fantasy is composed of seriousness and all joy borders on sorrow. The voyou is the human being in whom the two worlds of joy and sorrow are confused. . . .
>
> The voyou is the man who escapes from everything that normally holds back other men: studies, family, civic duties, religious duties. The voyou is the adventurer of space, of non-passable roads, of the immense freedom of cities and fields. (P. 81)

> The poet's departure is therefore a flight, an evasion, a seizure of the unreal (P. 84)

As decadents, Moydia and Katya may be seen, not just as superficial social butterflies, but more pertinently as seekers of knowledge in the role of voyou. Significantly, Moydia comments: "It's because we are so extravagant that we do not reach justice . . . we reach poetry" (p. 26, Barnes's ellipsis).

Generally, those who read the story as a chronicle of postwar malaise ignore differences between the sisters. Throughout the narration, Katya is reserved, accepting yet vaguely critical of her sister. Katya "lives more slowly"; she relates that "only women listen to me, but men adore Moydia. To her they do not listen, they look" (p. 24). When Moydia finally has a lover, "she laughed and cried, lying face down, and whimpering, 'Isn't it *wonderful!*' "

Katya observes without conviction, "And perhaps it was indeed wonderful, Madame." In this way their life is questioned, causing uncertainty for the reader. How *are* we to view their lives? If Katya's narration reveals reservations about Moydia's life, her participation in the decadent pose is nevertheless unqualified. She is very much part of the "well-planned life" in her dancing and in her desire for high-topped boots that recall her past and her father.

Katya's difference, however, is important. She is skeptical yet accepting, a participant but also an observer. Together they fit Fowlie's description of the clown/voyou. Moydia is the actor, poseur, charlatan, clown; Katya represents the opposite side, the silent observer, the poet who both participates and remains alone, in exile. Katya in observing and reporting becomes the artist, just as Vanka had, though here her voice is not memorializing, except in a very broad sense. Her voice, rather, is that of one who seeks to explain, to render intelligible life and its identity with death, that is, Moydia and her lover, who is "beastly with finis." The artist therefore is both part of life but also always an observer who creates a reality that is superior to life while also reflecting it. Seen from this perspective, the sisters are dual aspects of a single person.

The title reinforces this suggestion, for "The Grande Malade" alludes to a sick person, the great, or perhaps, the grown-up sick person. The title probably does not refer to Moydia's lover, the obvious choice, for *Grande* is feminine. Even though the feminine may be appropriate for the gay lover, as Moydia's lover, he has been referred to as "he" throughout the story. Therefore, the sick person may be either Moydia or Katya, or presumably both of them, as they portray tendencies within a single being. They represent, as "The Love Song of J. Alfred Prufrock" does, the objectification of two elements within a single person, perhaps that of the unspeaking Madame. One element experiences, the other observes and creates. From this perspective the action of the story is the acceptance of death and the necessity to create beautiful and well-planned lives. Whether the sisters succeed or not, the search itself is important. This theme, almost unnoticed beneath the surface, structures incident and character, giving both depth and complexity to the story.

With greater restraint and subtlety, Barnes handles the same theme, the symbolic encounter of imagination and external reality, in "The Passion," published in 1924 in *Transition* II. The story, whose progression of precise details creates a static effect, focuses on the life of the princess Frederica Rholinghausen. The omniscient narrator introduces readers to the princess through the ritual of her carriage rides through the park—daily except on Thursdays, when she receives guests. The opening establishes the ordered nature of her life and its slow retreat into a narrower and narrower center as she ages.

The princess herself is an admirable presence whose primary trait is her acceptance of mortality:

> At times, raising her eyeglasses at the uncompromising moment, she had surprisingly the air of a *gallant*, a *bon-vivant*—but there was a wash of blue in her flesh that spoke of the acceptance of mortality. She never spoke of the spirit. (P. 73)

Her Thursday visitors include solicitous aunts and an indifferent nephew whose actions suggest that a scrupulous interest in an inheritance motivates his visits. The other visitor, the important one, in terms of the subtle confrontation of values that the story relates, is Kurt Anders, who has visited the princess on the second Thursday of the month for thirty years. The description of Anders and the depiction of the relationship between Anders and the princess is developed through the balance of what "gossips" say and the narrator's countering assertion of the truth.

Anders is one who courts gossip and reputation in the world. A common figure in Barnes's fiction, he is known by gossips to have disappointed his family; he has associated with the "scion of the house of Valois," who is known as a modern but "could not keep away from museums or wax work, particularly the roped-off sections housing royal equipages" (p. 75). Anders has a sexual reputation with both men and women, but the narrator counters the romance of rumor with a view of the truth: "Anders enjoyed the manoeuvre, the perfected 'leap,' the trick pulled off, and the general sane weather" (p. 75). Anders spends his time walking in the park.

The same pattern of supposition is developed regarding the relationship of Anders and the princess. Some argue that the princess is the only real passion of his life, others that the princess's selfishness has prevented their union, yet others that they were "as good as husband and wife." The pattern of gossip and the return to purported reality at the narrator's observation is again repeated: "All of this was nonsense. They were pages in an old volume, brought together by the closing of the book" (p. 76).

The tone of the story supports this conclusion. The atmosphere describing their Thursdays suggests the warmth and longevity of a pleasant relationship. Anders speaks of autumn, cathedral architecture, drama, etchings, and "he would walk up and down before her until she noticed the pockets of his coat into which he had stuck small flowers" (p. 75). He talks of the "uses of the fool in Shakespeare": to this the princess, referring obliquely perhaps to Anders, comments on "the impracticability of maintaining tradition now that every man was his own fool" (p. 76).

Only in the last visit is there any suggestion of difficulty. The "strain" announced by the narrator involves opposed concepts of love. Anders claims that "walking straight up to dreadfulness . . . is love." The princess counters: "The last attendant on an old woman is always an 'incurable'." She then adds "with mordant acerbity," "But—if a little light man with a beard had said 'I love you,' I should have believed in God." The story concludes, "Shortly after, she did not live" (p. 76).

Apparently, the comment is directed to Anders, but in what sense can he be considered an incurable? Or his own fool, if the echo of the princess's comment carries that far? The remarks of the princess hint at her recognition that Anders has a reputation for "passionate risk" which he does not possess. Her comments seem to imply that Anders is willing to deceive himself, to believe in illusions. As his own fool, he lacks the sanitive influence recognized as one of the roles of the Shakespearean fool. Her observation affirms both her awareness of his emptiness, that is, his lightness, and yet reveals her love for him. Though her love has existed over the years, she recognizes his unsuitability in his posing and his worldliness. Her response is exile, but, unlike that of Lydia Passova in "Mother" (A Book), the exile of the princess seems an affirmation of mutually contradictory claims: those of Anders and the world, which are disappointing, and those of the imagination. Like Mageen in "At the Root of the Stars," the princess in exile retains the integrity of her imagination without degrading the claims of reality. She lives in the world but is not of it.

Two views of love are thus opposed: Anders's view, which, because of its romantic and desperate nature, remains unfulfilled, and that of the princess, whose statement implies that love is an earthly manifestation of God. In this sense she characterizes love as a spiritualizing force. Her concept of love is implied in the title of the story, "The Passion," which points to a paradox common to Barnes's work: passion is equally love and suffering. They are woven inextricably. In declaring that had she been told that Anders loved her she would have believed in God, the princess asserts the transcendent value of human love. The princess, however, lacking the experience of that kind of love, is admirable in the absolute accuracy of her perceptions and in her imaginative capacity to live without denying the reality of physical human nature. We are told, "Now it is said that the old cannot approach the grave without fearful apprehension or religious rite. The princess did" (p. 73). Not Madame von Bartmann, but the princess is one of Barnes's finest women. She embodies a strength of character and imagination that Barnes herself must have found worthy.

In the necessary silence Barnes set out the "abundant inadequacies of life"; she exploited brief situations, extravagant characters, and elusive prose to suggest both the desire for meaning and purpose and the difficulty of securing that desire. Yet the sturdiness of spirit of Julie and the princess is a compliment to human consciousness and a contrast to the enervating fatalism of Madame von Bartmann and Gaya; Katya and Moydia testify also to the desire for life and meaning. As in the journalism and drama, conscious living is the necessary condition of human life; yet in her world of fiction Barnes recognized also that consciousness itself was a fragile and painful proposition and that meaning was elusive. This is what she lamented, not consciousness itself.

4
The Vanity of Ryder's Race

Djuna Barnes's first novel, *Ryder,* perplexed its early reviewers. Responses ranged from the *American Mercury* view, "a piece of rubbish," to L. Calhoun's thoughtful summation, which, touching also upon Barnes's own character, points to *Ryder's* diversity:

> Now, in Paris, . . . Djuna Barnes has written a book that is all that she was, and must still be—vulgar, beautiful, defiant, witty, poetic, and a little mad—a bewildering hodge-podge of the obscene and virginal, of satire and wistfulness, of the grossest humor and the most delicate sadness—a book that absolutely baffles classification, but that surely is a most amazing thing to have come from a woman's hand.[1]

Disparate elements are so pervasive in *Ryder* that reviewers and critics have questioned its thematic unity and the outcome of its action. Some reviewers found the book a good-humored portrayal of Wendell Ryder, who "loved all womankind and loved them well." C. Hartley Grattan observed, "She has written a highly sophisticated and amusing hymn to the inherent lustiness of mankind." L. B. wrote that *Ryder* "is really a tragedy of women."[2] However, a hymn "to the inherent lustiness of mankind" suggests a very different reading from one that views the book as a "tragedy of women." In the biography, *Djuna,* Andrew Field argued that the book is highly autobiographical and drew parallels between Wendell Ryder and Barnes's father, adding that "Miss Barnes hated her father."[3] The biographical information suggests that a reading which sees Wendell as an embodiment of heroic masculine principle may be a misreading—a result, perhaps, of overemphasizing the narrative line to the exclusion of the digressive material, which creates the effect of multiple chords. By exploiting juxtapositions of characters and themes, Barnes achieves double meanings. For example, the character of Wendell Ryder seems positive, yet as she had in the journalism, Barnes orchestrates criticism of Ryder's character.

Thus, even though the diversity of *Ryder* seemed new in comparison to the style and techniques of the short stories that had appeared in the decades before the publication of *Ryder,* the newness is a matter of degree rather than one of kind. For in *Ryder* Barnes relies on contrasting moods, styles, themes, and on an intricate structure built upon digressions and a series of debates. And all are familiar techniques in the journalism and fiction (though used more sparingly) to achieve double meaning or to undercut an apparent surface meaning. And in *Ryder* we find Barnes's ongoing exploitation of social satire and her concern with the human spirit.

Barnes's apparent aims in *Ryder* are twofold. The first level is social: she satirizes middle-class conformity and sexual repressiveness. At this level Wendell Ryder is a rather appealing nonconformist who challenges the orthodoxy of society. For example, Scott identifies the theme of *Ryder* as "a developing conflict between social 'propriety' and Wendell's unorthodox life style." He concludes: "The book argues, in effect, that, disjointed and peculiar as Ryder's life appears, it is closer to nature than more conventional lives; that such a life is more spontaneous, more joyous, and far more productive of beauty."[4] However, Barnes is also interested in human consciousness, and in *Ryder* her second aim is to present the perpetual conflict between physical nature and the human spirit in terms of the innocent, that is, unconscious, egotism of Wendell Ryder. Essentially, the organizing idea of the book is the sufficiency of Wendell Ryder, whose devotion to physical being is symbolized by his polygamist philosophy, a philosophy that also identifies him with procreation and death. However, the negative aspects of Ryder have not been generally recognized, partly because of *Ryder's* elaborate structure and partly because of the surface charm of Wendell Ryder.

Irreverent and likeable, Ryder is an outlaw—opposed to the repressiveness of society. He goes about the neighborhood asserting a polygamist philosophy that mocks middle-class sexual beliefs. He wishes his children to grow up free of social and sexual repression; therefore, he educates his growing family at home. When he encounters objections from the school board, he meets their inquiries with an attack upon the conditions of the school and its well, pointing out that as a citizen he will demand a new well be dug and pure water supplied: "Ryder as an outlaw is less trouble than citizen Ryder," he warns.[5] He argues the similarity of animal nature and human nature with respect to sexuality: "What is this swims like dregs within the truth / That animal and man be set apart? / I hear not muchë difference in the heart / That beatës soft and constant under hide, / And this same hammer ticking in my side!" (p. 77). Both he and his mother Sophia represent a humorous and open acceptance of sexual nature, though she finds her son's devotion to procreation "past comprehension." When he asks, "What does one do with nature?" Sophia answers wryly, "A humane man would occasionally give it respite" (p. 226).

But if Ryder's character represents a criticism of the sexual attitudes of society, Barnes also undermines this character much as she had that of Wilson Mizner in her early *Telegraph* feature. Thus, even though Ryder's polygamist philosophy mocks middle-class reticence and sexual practice, his middle-class roots are apparent nevertheless. Ryder's sexuality is in the service of procreation, that ever present middle-class duty, though the exaggeration of his sexuality for comic effect initially obscures this fact. Chapter 10, for example, describes Wendell's dream of having as many children as the number of chess pieces, then as many as the number of cards in a deck. Readers may see this as merely comic, but Barnes turns the comedy to irony. While his extraordinary service to procreation is comic, more important is that this devotion masks his fear of death. As a begetter of children, Ryder is identified with the procreative principle, which, through various digressions, is associated with death. Thus, after initially leading a reader to share Ryder's perspective, Barnes calls Ryder's values into question.

The methods that Barnes uses to question Ryder's values derive from early practices of juxtaposing themes and characters, but in *Ryder* she extends the practice through her use of the anatomy form. In *Anatomy of Criticism* Northrop Frye discussed many of the features that are apparent in *Ryder*: a "digressing narrative"; symposium discussions, or dialogue forms; "mixtures of verse and prose"; catalogues; and a tendency to *melos*, or metrical elements in prose; "stylizing of characters along 'humor' lines; and ridicule of philosophers and pendants."[6] In *Ryder* Barnes uses these devices not only to question Ryder's life but also to question whether a life can adequately be represented in a linear fashion and whether there is value in such representation. As J.-K. Huysmans and Gourmont had declared, naturalistic depiction of a life seemed a dead end.

While one might hesitiate to suggest that all the disparate material can be successfully related to a single pattern, much of the disparate material of *Ryder* questions the values of Ryder. Wendell's conversation with the stiltsman, for example, seems an arbitrary interruption of the narrative, yet the dialogue relates to the underlying theme of identity, achievement, and betrayal, even as it complicates the surface level of the work. The stiltsman, playing on the idea that an arch honors the achievements of man, declares: "In like manner I, poor Tom, do erect myself to myself, as it is not likely that by other than my own achievements I shall reach that pinnacle of renown." And he adds, "Everything is true that is honoured" (p. 24). Ryder's curious response to this declaration, "I fled you down the arches of the years," is a misquote from Francis Thompson's "Hound of Heaven": I fled Him, down the arches of the years." The difference between the two passages is that one suggests secular identity, the other Christ as Hound of Heaven. Both contexts imply that Ryder's giving in to his nature is a flight from something—achievement, or perhaps the identity of self that the stiltsman asserts by "erecting himself to himself." On another level Ryder's allusion, whether conscious or not, points to his denial of the life of the spirit. A possible source for the stiltsman's allusion reinforces this theme: "Unless above himself he can Erect himself, how poor a thing is man."[7]

In *Ryder* Barnes uses a mixture of verse and prose to raise doubts about Wendell's ideas and conduct. For example, in Chapter 10, written in heroic couplets, Ryder is identified with sensuality and death; begetting children is seen as a kind of futile game: "Though all, alas, in time unto the tombs / The game must go . . ." (p. 69). The same chapter presents what seems an unrelated matter, Ryder's fastidiousness: "To this exceeding niceness had he groped / Out of a still small voice which said: 'No pains / Can be too cunning where dame nature reigns' " (p. 76). His fastidiousness is obsessive and comic, a sign of his refusal to accept mortality.

In the same chapter, Ryder's identification with animal nature to justify his unrestrained sexuality is drawn to its logical and ironic conclusion. Barnes shows that while Ryder identifies with animal nature to justify his sensuality, he nevertheless maintains, as did the middle class, his superiority to animal nature by virtue of reason. In this context a fairly perplexing digression becomes intelligible. Barnes, in presenting Ryder's attempt to teach animals to speak, particularly his horse His-olodalgus, creates a comic situation that demonstrates Ryder's kinship with animal nature as well as his failure to understand the full implications of that identity. Ryder, having determined that "nothing so out-flares / And brings to speech, as flattery of breed," praises his animals so that they might speak and avoid slaughter. He reasons that man will hesitate to slaughter that which speaks in his own tongue. Barnes's humor here is fantastic and disconcerting. She has joined a humorous innocence in Wendell's character with a satiric thrust at human vulnerability to flattery. More biting is the irony that humankind indeed does not hesitate to take the lives of those humans who speak the same language. The final irony, of course, is that while Ryder identifies with animal nature with respect to sexuality, he fails to comprehend that mortality rides mankind as well.

The heroic verse of this chapter is particularly effective in undermining Ryder's heroic pretensions as father and philosopher. The verse increases Dan Wendell's stature, but only to undermine comically this "legendary" figure. While the verse implies Ryder's heroism, his deeds are not only comic but often ludicrous, such as the attempt to teach animals to speak. The heroic verses that refer to Ryder's fastidiousness are not only bawdy, but they reduce his stature to physical being. Thus, the disparity between the middle English verse form and the mundane details should warn readers that despite the humor there is an element of foolishness about this rather likeable character.

Important to the criticism of Ryder and his philosophy are various digressions that associate Ryder with procreation and death. The connections are implied rather than stated directly. By disrupting the story of Ryder's life and its satiric aim, these chapters create thematic echoes that insinuate Ryder's inadequacies.

Chapter 19, for example, "Amelia and Kate Taken to Bed," relates in a fairly straightforward fashion that both Kate-Careless and Amelia gave birth on the same day. Amelia's child is a boy, Kate's a girl. Wendell's elaborate dressing of a child is described in Chapter 21, "Wendell Dresses His Child." His elaborate care, the infant's stillness, and the repetition of the phrase, "that it knew not joy or sorrow separately, for that it was born feet first, amid wailing and crying and great lamentation, from the midst of its mother" warn that the infant may be stillborn. Only in Chapter 22, "And Amelia Sings a Lullaby," is the death of Kate's child confirmed indirectly by Amelia's reference to a lost child and a woman's sorrow. Her lullaby characterizes birth as passing through "the world's gate," which, as it can refer to death as well as birth, conflates the two.

The lullaby relates Amelia's feeling that life is a mixed blessing, given its trouble, and that death may not be a bitter thing. Though some readers have seen the lullaby as indicative of Amelia's hatred for Kate, details of the passage suggest the possibility that Amelia's song reflects her attitude about death in general. Furthermore, Amelia's basic decency is commended by Kate when she confronts Wendell and his mother.

A troublesome point, however, is Ryder's solicitous care for the dead (or dying) infant. Barnes's elaborate and heavily cadenced prose and the ritualistic manner in which Wendell dresses the child (p. 129) create a sense of confusion in the reader. Some of this confusion is generated by the conflicting moods: an understandable sorrow at the infant's early death, but also a sense of excessive sorrow created by the elaborate prose and by the contrast between Amelia's resignation and Wendell's attitude toward both infants. The dead child is Ryder's, as the chapter title indicates. He has, however, questioned the paternity of Amelia's son because of its dark color, until O'Connor observes, "Bile alone is father of its colour" (p. 121). In effect, because of the elaborate prose and the identification of Wendell with the dead child, Wendell is associated with death.

In these chapters Barnes explores Ryder's character in order not only to comment satirically on social taboos, particularly with respect to sexual conventions, but also to show the limited values of Ryder's views. On the surface, he is associated with a zesty love of live, but to the extent that he is identified with an exaggerated procreative principle, the pattern becomes complicated. Beneath the surface lust for life is the corollary connection with fear, indecisiveness, and death. He tells Dr. O'Connor that he breeds children so that he may come to memory from time to time. Lacking a belief in a transcendent God and the life of the spirit, he plans a sort of immortality through his children.

The Debates of Ryder

Qualification of Ryder's character and aims is carried out most humorously in a series of debates in which Ryder's character is measured against adversity and found wanting. The series begins with Chapter 8, "Pro and Con, or the Sisters Louise," which is an abstract statement of Wendell's suitability. This idea is then examined in the epistolary debate between Amelia and her sister Anne. Ryder's dialogues with Molly Dance, Laura Twelvetrees, Lady Bridesleep, and Dr. Connor conclude the series.

The sisters Louise play no active role in the narrative line; the purpose of the chapter is tangential commentary, establishing the universal context for the reader's acceptance of Ryder as representative of human nature. The sisters face each other, playing a piano duet, while they discuss the uses of adversity (p. 48). The subject of their rather ribald debate is Wendell Ryder. One sister, presumably Pro, offers "that never man before so thoroughly enjoyed his parts, so trusted to them, and so managed them that . . . others trust in like measure." Her sister, arguing the Con position, admits a "floating doubt as to the ultimate importance, shall I say, satisfaction, of man to the mass, when . . . the mass is female and the man is Wendell." The issue is then rephrased as whether the "nature in one man can be perpetual." Her sister, Pro concludes, "Hardly perpetual, but perhaps recurringly satisfactory" (p. 49).

Along with the sexual innuendoes run the themes of trust and the permanence of life itself in the individual. The sister, Con, who doubts man's "importance," and specifically Wendell's, tells a parable of a world order where women live in harmony until the appearance of Ryder sets them against one another: "Writhing, biting, tearing, scratching, screaming, crying, over and over they rolled, in blood and tears. . . . and down, down into the valley's bottomless depth, now she on top, now she, now she under, now she, and into the ravine at last, where between tall rank grasses the rubbish blooms." The sister, ostensibly Pro, asks, "Do they return?" Con answers, "Does Hell spew out its damned? It does."

When her sister asks whether they should "encompass a return," the sister Con, who has created the parable of the fall, replies, "My dear, stir up the fire for tea, and remember that Hell is not for ladies" (p. 51). In short, the resolution is against the cycle of life represented by Ryder, namely, birth and death. The sister Con argues against this kind of adversity: "Hell is not for ladies."

In the following chapter a debate similar to that of the sisters Louise ends differently. Do what she can to dissuade Amelia, Anne loses her sister to Wendell. Anne and Amelia are interesting emotional counterpoints to the sisters Louise. Ann (Con) is a pessimist; she has jilted three men because none is worthy. Amelia (Pro) is the naive optimist, a willing believer, who suggests that Anne's wisdom is not wisdom, but fear: "'Tis because you are too fearful . . . and no sooner see a touch of green but do think the whole man a little game" (p. 64).

Amelia's name suggests the alternative she chooses, for "Amelia" literally means "diligent" and reaches back to the Germanic base, *amal*, meaning "work" or "trouble." In pulling Ryder off the wall and into her "inner courtyard," Amelia accepts adversity, the cycle of life, activity, and struggle. Those traits go with her throughout *Ryder*, for she is the worker. Neither Kate-Careless nor Ryder shares her diligence.

These thematic strands—adversity and Ryder's suitability—are extended into his encounter with neighborhood women who challenge his assumption that he and his philosophy are able to meet adversity. In these affairs, the women willingly and humorously accept him as a lover, while simultaneously rejecting his procreative philosophy. In each situation, as in the meeting with Laura Twelvetrees, Ryder asserts his aim to father exceptional children who will grow up independent of the values of society and testify to his values in doing so. His encounters with Molly Dance and Lady Bridesleep, however, demonstrate not only the shortsightedness of his philosophy but, in a sense, its very commonness, its middle-class quality.

Perhaps only Molly Dance offers a genuine parallel to Wendell Ryder in terms of her procreative propensities. Molly Dance might well represent Rémy de Gourmont's principle that one has an "inalienable right to interpret the world in whatever way one pleased."[8] Her cosmology, to Ryder's consternation, is an inventive and irreverent takeoff on traditional middle-class beliefs. Original sin, for example, in Molly's understanding, was not woman's but man's: "It was an apple, surely, but man it was who snapped it up, scattering the seeds, and these he uses to this day to get his sons by" (p. 259). Revealing an enormous capacity for life, plus humor and imagination, Molly Dance is completely amoral. As a dog breeder, she exercises rare caution with respect to the mating of her dogs; however, as the narrator relates, "Molly, it must be writ, was no better than her dogs, and seldom as good, for she got her children where and when it pleased her" (p. 249). Wendell inquires if she knows who is the father of her last born. Molly replies, "who cares? He didn't, I don't, and the child won't have to, and that's simplification" (p. 260). Ryder offers to establish certainty in the matter by fathering her next child, and Molly agrees amiably enough. Afterward, however, she observes, "there's only one thing that might make something uncertain of this certainty." She explains that the issue is "whether the child shall know you for its father or no," adding that two nights ago the corner policeman had the same idea. And that, Molly muses, "only goes to show you that one man's thoughts are not worth much more than another's" (p. 261). On two levels Ryder's ideas are shaken: in his pride of fatherhood and in his estimation of his own personal importance.

Ryder's encounter with Lady Bridesleep is a variation of his encounter with Laura Twelvetrees, who has asserted the "aristocracy of no outcome." The difference between the two women is that Lady Bridesleep is well into her sixties and therefore past childbearing age, a fact that Ryder fails to notice. Characterized as an epicure and one who was "pleased by nature at its most natural," Lady Bridesleep embodies Gourmont's argument, in "Dissociation of Ideas," that all varieties of human sexuality are natural, denying the claims of religious moralists who argued that certain forms of sexuality were "against nature" and that sexual pleasure and procreation were necessarily linked. In Lady Bridesleep, we see the voluptuary, who, because of her age, represents the separation of carnal pleasure from the procreative duty.

When Ryder asks when they shall name the child he imagines Lady Bridesleep has conceived, she replies, "Nothing and Never. . . . He shall accomplish all the others leave undone. You need No Child also, my good man, all fathers have one. On him you shall hang that part of your ambition too heavy for mortal" (p. 279). Obliquely, the experience points toward the vanity of all mortal ambitions, though Ryder does not yet perceive the significance of Lady Bridesleep's message. Here Ryder is ridiculed not for his apparently unlimited sensuality, which is matched by that of Lady Bridesleep, but for the extravagant claims he makes for his own "satisfactoriness," which is to be exemplified by his children. Both encounters point to the futility of Ryder's procreative philosophy as a means of justifying his existence. What remains is his discovery of the vulnerability of the self he has created.

Ryder's Vulnerability

Ryder's vulnerability is foreshadowed as he talks with his mother of his response to Oscar Wilde, whose fate anticipates Ryder's own. Though he regarded Wilde as a man of beauty and imagination, Ryder recalls seeing Wilde and turning away from him:

> The scandal had burst, and though he was the core, the fragrant centre of a rousing stench, in a month he was a changed man, not changing, sitting within his cell, weeping, writing, plotting "De Profundis," his fingers outside his mouth, shuddering in all his soft female body, direct suffering in his breasts; a bull caught and captured, sentenced, hamstrung, marauded, peered at, peeped upon, regarded and discovered to be a gentle sobbing cow, giving self-suck at the fountain of self, that he might die in his own image, a soft pain chartered she, a girl cast out of heaven, harnessed for a stallion's turn; tremolo to his own swan song. I turned away and was matchlessly damned. (P. 218)

This passage is interesting because its style is particularly appropriate to Ryder's narcissistic musing and because it implies a thematic parallel between Ryder and Wilde. Constructed on elaborate parallel phrases, the linear movement is held together loosely with semi-colons. Identified as loose style by Morris W. Croll, in *"Attic" & Baroque Style*, the passage depends upon asymmetrical techniques, including length of phrases, or movement by a series of metaphorical leaps. In this passage, Ryder, as speaker, moves through a series of predicate nouns, from "man" in the first series, through "bull," "pain-chartered she," "girl," to "tremolo." The progression of the sentence is not logical; rather the reader is forced to make imaginative connections between the items in the series."[9] In this process the reader recreates Ryder's imaginative perception of Wilde's changing self-concept.

The effect of such a style, in Croll's view, is to present the prose of an "animated talker"; its purpose, "to portray a mind thinking," not necessarily the reasoned and formally shaped thought itself. The series of adjectives, "caught and captured, sentenced, hamstrung, marauded,

peered at, peeped upon . . ." expresses not only Ryder's latent fear of
social scrutiny but equally the fear of self-scrutiny, leading to a self-
image less pleasing than what he normally projects and enjoys; thus the
animated talker conceals from himself and others an undesirable self—
but ironically in talking betrays himself. The prose is strangely appropriate to Ryder's situation: that is, his talk simultaneously reveals and
obscures himself to himself and to readers.

Ryder has created an image of himself as a father and enlightened
social rebel, a role which justifies his existence in his own eyes and
simultaneously feeds his vanity. However, the fragility of this self-
shaped identity is illustrated by thematic ties between Ryder and Oscar
Wilde. With the identification of Ryder and Wilde, two themes come
together: physicial nature and sexuality and the created self. The significance of these themes within the structure of the book is apparent if we
consider *Ryder* from a symbolic perspective.

The Symbolic Context

The symbolic level of *Ryder* is set in the opening chapter, "Jesus
Mundane," a puzzling chapter as it bears no apparent relationship to
those that follow: the story of Sophia's parents, Sophia's chamberpots,
and Wendell's birth. "Jesus Mundane" is a direct address, though the
identities of who is addressed and who is speaking are never disclosed.
The reader is forced to assume that some spirit is addressed by some
Creator and the spirit descends to the world to be born. That much can
be ascertained through the implied parallel with Jesus announced in the
chapter's title. The spirit is advised, "Go not with fanatics," who are
distracted with the end of life, but "Go, thou, then, to lesser men, who
have for all things unfinished and uncertain, a great capacity. . . . Thy
rendez-vous is not with the Last Station, but with small comforts, like to
apples in the hand, and small cups quenching . . ." (p. 1). The speaker
seems to imply that the business of humankind is with physical reality.
Furthermore, uncertainty and ignorance are man's initial condition.
What has gone before is unknown: "These things are as the back of thy
hand to three. Thou hast not seen them" (p. 5).

Despite its obscurity, the direct address establishes a context which
indicates that at one level the character of Wendell Ryder is to be read
symbolically as representative of mankind in general. The opening invites the reader to trace the progress of the spirit who descends to the
trial of existence. If the opening establishes the context of a symbolic
trial, then the repeated question of the conclusion—"And whom should
he disappoint now?"—suggests the failure of Wendell Ryder. The nature

of the failure is confirmed by the symbolic details of his unusual costume.

Ryder, who dresses in green and has white rats about him when Amelia first sees him, shares this rather eccentric trait and others with the father of the three boys in Barnes's early drama, *Three from the Earth.* In that drama, the father, alluded to by Kate and the three boys, is revealed to have a weak stomach and to have been a country philosopher of sorts; he has tried to be perfect, failed, and ended up by slitting his own throat because "everything"—a fat wife who has been a prostitute, Kate whom he has loved, and the three boys—has been "too much" for him.

Ryder shares with his prototype his polygamous household, his weak stomach, and his philosophical bent, but their common penchant for green clothing and white rats is perhaps the most striking similarity.[10] J. E. Cirlot notes in *A Dictionary of Symbols* that green, as associated with the sixth enigma of the tarot pack, The Lover, is identified with "indecision," "uncertainty and temptation."[11] The sixth enigma itself refers to the legend of Hercules who was given the choice of two women: "the one personifying Virtue (or decisive activity, vocation, sense of purpose, and struggle) and the other Vice (passive-ness, surrender to base impulses and to external pressures)." The dress of the tarot lover is particolored, red and green, red for activity and green for indecision; Ryder's red hair can be seen perhaps as substitute for the original parti-colored dress. The other significant detail of Ryder's dress, as it is described, is the presence of white rats. Again, Cirlot records that rats are associated with "infirmity and death. . . . a phallic implication has been superimposed . . . but only in so far as it is dangerous or repugnant."

Thus, Ryder's green clothing and his subsequent choice of Kate-Careless are symbolic. Given Amelia's association with work and striving and the acceptance of adversity, Ryder's choice of the fleshy and passive Kate-Careless—indifference itself, a fact of her allegorical name—confirms his surrender to "base impulses and external pressures." His life is an evasion, for rather than cultivate a self-awareness adequate to accept mortality and the limitation of physical nature he has surrendered to physical nature, evading spiritual potential. This is apparent when, confronted by the angry townspeople who demand that he choose between Kate and Amelia, he acknowledges to his mother Sophia: "I have unfathered myself" (p. 318). He has given up self-direction for social controls. In such a context, the possibilities that the stiltsman has offered in the beginning become comically relevant, for Ryder has operated at the level of the pun which the stiltsman offered, but in doing so he has, in another sense, failed to "erect himself to himself."

The final chapter concludes with repetitions of the phrase, "And whom should he disappoint now?" Ryder is sitting in a field surrounded by animals:

> And everything and its shape became clear in the dark, by tens and tens they ranged, and lifted their lids and looked at him; in the air and in the trees and on the earth and from under the earth, and regarded him long, and he forbore to hide his face. They seemed close ranged, and now they seem far ranged, and they moved now near, now far, as a wave comes and goes, and they lifted their lids and regarded him, and spoke not in their many tongues, and they went a far way, and there was a little rest, and they came close, and there was none. Closing in about him nearer, and swinging out wide and from him far, and came in near and near, and as a wave, closed over him, and he drowned, and arose while ye yet might go.
> And whom should he disappoint? (P. 323)

Rich with ambiguity, the image identifies Ryder's character metaphorically with nature and self-consuming concern. He is surrounded by animals, that is, limited to natural, instinctual reality. The wavelike motion, apparent in the animals' eyes that advance, accusingly, and recede, giving rest, evokes the water image wherein Narcissus saw himself reflected. Significantly, drowning suggests a surrender to self. His capitulation to social demands represents his failure to forge truth and values for himself, just as his capitulation to physical desires represents a denial of the spirit.

Nevertheless, in Ryder's character, Barnes achieves an objectivity that does not condemn, for he remains an amiable character, though the series of debates necessarily qualify his views. Yet because he fails to create a truth that goes beyond simple rebellion against the restrictive codes of society, readers experience a feeling of disappointment and also sympathy. The mingling of moods that pervades the book achieves a distancing effect so that we recognize in Ryder the human condition: uncertain and beleaguered from within and without by conflicting desires.

The Alternative to Ryder

In *Ryder* Barnes has created a work that dramatizes her concerns with morality, identity, and conscious awareness! In doing so, she has made these concerns the inconspicuous organizing principle of the work. On one level, *Ryder* appears to be a protest against a repressive middle-class ethic, yet on the symbolic level, the work conveys a considerably more complex idea. The principle of sensual reality is never denied; it is, however, presented as limited, yet powerful in distorting human nature. Barnes's point here is that human nature is not limited to physical reality. O'Connor, Julie, and Elisha testify to the spiritual dimension of human nature.

O'Connor, as a sensual being, is acutely aware of the pleasures of the flesh, and, as a physician, of human suffering and the fragility of human life. Subject to the conflicting claims of the senses and also aware of a desire not to be subject to the senses only, he represents the perpetual conflict between physical nature and the needs of the human spirit. He recognizes both the insufficiency and the necessity of the sensual reality. O'Connor's experience convinces him that one cannot trust nature, the sensual reality alone, though this is what Ryder has done, elevating his own physical nature to a philosophy.

While O'Connor never achieves the purity and serenity he desires, the strength of his sensual drive and its nature—O'Connor is a homosexual, a form of sexuality the middle-class considered "unnatural" and degenerate—convince him of his subjugation to the flesh, thereby providing the impetus that necessitates reasoned control, that is, manners, God, or moral behavior, something to regulate the instincts. He is, therefore, like Wendell Ryder in terms of instinctual nature, but while O'Connor recognizes the need for control (success is something else), Ryder rationalizes his nature through his philosophy extolling instinct.

In addition to the point of view represented by O'Connor, the perspectives of Ryder's children provide alternative views that qualify those of Wendell Ryder. Both Elisha and Julie reject Ryder's ways. Though our view of Julie is a series of glimpses, these disclosures show she is different and special. Julie attacks Kate for lying when Elisha strikes her brother Hannel, seeing her not as the disease, but as "the manifestation of such emanating directly from her father" (p. 183). Even though her grandmother loves Julie best, Sophia has a difficult relationship with her because of Julie's independence. Knowing that she herself is not as grand as she appears, Sophia lies, thinking: "the thing I've seemed will balance the account." It does—almost, for Julie, recognizing the lies, later sees them as the best of a "capacious soul." Yet Julie prefers truth.

Julie is a shadowy figure whose implications as a character are illuminated when one considers them in the context of O'Connor's discussion with one of Ryder's sons. In response to the boy's cynical belief that there is no point in any activity, O'Connor asserts the value of the activity for its own sake:

> You get no more good by diligent thought than another by no thought at all, saving the thought which you have, and he has not,

and while 'tis true that you must give it up at death and loose it on the wind again, like a caged pigeon, it was yours once, and may go croaking of the difference, with somewhat of your voice, to be heard by yet another ear, for a remembrance. (P. 307)

O'Connor's image describes the practice of generation by ideas, an activity that characterizes the role of the artist. Hence the importance of Julie's difference. As she stands apart from the family and as she recognizes her grandmother's willingness to put the best face on things as a betrayal and an achievement, she surpasses both Sophia and Wendell.

Elisha too stands outside the family and is identified as artistic because of his skill in playing the piano. He shares with Julie her respect for truth, having interrupted the fight among Kate, Amelia, and Julie to confess that he has "chiseled Hannel's head," and his mother is a liar for denying it. Now, years later, as he prepares to play for the townspeople, he "bends over . . . he is with himself alone, he has thrown off the people, a drowning mass about a drowning man's neck, and plays loud, and is liberated to himself, softly, softly for my soul's sake, says he, and plays softly" (p. 296). Elisha's way, "playing for his soul's sake," testifies to the human potential of the artist for liberating the soul from subjection to the physical being.

Through O'Connor, Julie, and Elisha, Barnes introduces a theme of the human spirit that balances physical nature. The comment of André Gide, a symbolist early in his career, is interesting in this context. In his *Journals* Gide wrote:

> I am torn by a conflict between the rules of morality and the rules of sincerity. Morality consists in substituting for the natural creature (the old Adam) a fiction that you prefer. But then you are no longer sincere. The old Adam is the sincere man.
> This occurs to me: the old Adam is the poet. The new man, whom you prefer, is the artist. The artist must take the place of the poet. From the struggle between the two is born the work of art. . . .[12]

The poet, then, represents experience, the realm of physical reality, but the artist, conscious decision. The work of art represents a precarious balance, a sacrifice of instinctual life but also a gain drawn from the conflict. A good is born from evil, in the sense that Baudelaire saw poetry as a redemptive act, the flowers that bloom from evil.

As in many of the short stories, the symbolic level is incorporated into the structure of *Ryder.* Beneath the surface complexity of *Ryder* and its level of social satire of middle-class values, the organizing principle of the work is the conflict between physical nature and the human spirit, an idea that has pervaded Barnes's early work from the interviews and one-acts, to the short stories of the Paris years.

In *Ryder* brief incidents used to vary the tone of the work and thematic parallels to qualify the character of Wendell Ryder produce a complicated texture that gives *Ryder* a sense of fullness—and a deceptive feeling of movement. A great many incidents are likely to create a feeling of activity as opposed to the slow, steady development of a single narrative line. In fact, the sense of activity belies the stasis at the heart of *Ryder*. The interaction of the household and Ryder's many affairs produces little in the way of crisis and denouement—repetitiveness is the primary fact of this world. The denouement comes from outside the basic action when Ryder is somewhat arbitrarily forced to choose between Kate and Amelia. Though Ryder fails to order his life, the reader confronts the disorder of Ryder's life. From the whirlpool of incidents, themes, parallel motifs, digressions, and debates, the reader provides the interpreting intelligence. Balance is necessary. The diversity of *Ryder* demands, in effect, that the reader achieve a balance, or understanding, through the complexity of *Ryder's* surface.

"A Trade too tender for Oblivion": Ryder's Daughter, Evangeline Musset

Ladies Almanack, published in November 1928, is a deliberate answer, or companion, to *Ryder*, published in August 1928. In *Ladies Almaneck*, Barnes uses the almanack form and notoriously ambiguous prose to serve multiple purposes. First, the humorous and explicit sexuality of *Ladies Almanack* continues Barnes's attack on middle-class sensibilities. Second, she satirizes lesbian love as sharing the same faults of heterosexual love. In this way she both legitimizes lesbian love and simultaneously demonstrates its limitations. Finally, Barnes is able to raise issues concerning spiritual well-being indirectly because the almanack tradition counterpoints seasonal time with the stages of human life. Thus, as in *Ryder*, Barnes contrasts the limitation of physical nature to the life of the superior sensibility represented by the artist.

Thematic considerations suggest that connections between *Ryder* and *Ladies Almanack* are conscious. In *Ryder*, "Three Great Moments of History" are told by Doctor O'Connor to one of Ryder's illegitimate sons who rejects his father's procreative philosophy. In *Ladies Almanack* the "Fourth Great Moment of History" is told to Evangeline Musset by Doll Furious who reminds Musset that she has undoubtedly heard the other three. Figuratively, the parallel suggests that Evangeline replaces the son.

This connection is strengthened by a conversation in *Ryder* between Wendell and his mother. Sophia dismisses Wendell's theory that his daughter Julie will be able to "get back" to him, meaning, presumably, be as he is. Sophia asserts instead that Julie will "go beyond" him. In *Ladies Almanack* Evangeline, figuratively the descendant of Ryder, does just that. Her messianic zeal in converting women to her creed parallels Ryder's espousal of his procreative philosophy, but because she advocates love of woman for woman, her actions parody his; therefore, she "goes beyond" him.

In addition, Evangeline surpasses Ryder in another way. She is identified with the Garden of Venus as opposed to the Camp of Nature, associated with heterosexual love, which Ryder represents. The image of the cultivated garden implies that lesbian love is to be preferred because it is "artificial," created, in contrast to what is "natural" and consequently base: heterosexual love. Such a reversal, reflecting the symbolist and decadent roots of Barnes's fiction, parodies middle-class sexual attitudes, which included the belief that forms of love other than heterosexual and procreative were perverse.[1] However, the approval given to Evangeline Musset is undercut, though she is neither denied nor exactly condemned: the Garden of Venus, though cultivated and artificial, is yet subject to time and decay.

The form of the work, the almanack, is peculiarly suited to Barnes's orchestration of multiple aims. As early as the 1640s, English almanack tradition was a "forum for the discussion of major contemporary issues."[2] Thus, though printed privately with limited distribution, *Ladies Almanack* takes up the very contemporary and controversial issue of lesbianism.[3] Paradoxically, a measure of Barnes's success in carrying out conflicting goals is demonstrated by the differences in critical opinion regarding the aim of the book. Barnes's foreword announces *Ladies Almanack* as "this slight satiric wigging," which literally means censure, or scolding. Nevertheless, critics have been uncertain in their response to this work. For example, Scott and Kannenstine took Barnes's foreword as a sign that censure was directed against lesbianism. Scott saw the book as urging "a sensible restraint against self-indulgence in the liberated Paris of the 1920s," adding that "it celebrated at the same time the lesbian coterie it appeared to scold."[4] Kannenstine read the book as a satire "on the notion of a cultural aristocracy of women with its rituals and credos, its chic, and its intrigues, its esoteric predispositions." He questioned whether it was a Sapphic manifesto or a "lamentation amid laughter." Finally, he saw in the work the theme of modern degradation: "Beneath its surface levity it is a pain-racked comedy, aware of a lost Eden and a confused present."[5]

In the biography Andrew Field followed Scott and Kannenstine in his estimate that the work "presents itself as a protest against the indelicacy of sexual manners of the time." However, he also reported Barnes's announcement to her friends: "I am writing the female Tom Jones," a comment that invites us to see the positive nature of the heroine Evangeline Musset.[6] Indeed, Susan Sniader Lanser argued that the work was a celebration of lesbianism. She commented that both Scott and Kannenstine overlook "the lesbian pleasures" of the book. In her view the work is "an inside joke" written for Natalie Clifford Barney and her lesbian friends.[7]

Certainly Lanser is correct; though *Ladies Almanack* treats certain lesbian ideas humorously, for example, the argument for lesbian marriage advanced by Lady Buck-and-Balk and Tilly-Tweed-in-Blood, it is not a full-scale censure of lesbianism per se. However, the work is not limited to a celebration of lesbianism. The work explores not just lesbian or heterosexual love but the limitations of physical love as opposed to such characteristic virtues as wisdom and stoic indifference. Thus, the theme of *Ladies Almanack* unites Barnes's decadent interest in the perverse with her symbolist concern for individual consciousness and mortality. Furthermore, one can hardly speak of this work without considering the bawdiness of Barnes's humor, which, in itself, is a satiric attack on middle-class propriety and sexual reticence. Much of Barnes's salacious humor seems designed purely to outrage.

To challenge traditional sexual ideas, Barnes exploited the moral force of the saint's life as a witness to a faith, even though the faith Evangeline Musset advocates is a reversal of the traditional "martyrdom of the senses." The heroine Evangeline Musset is described as "one Grande Red Cross for the Pursuance, the Relief, and the Distraction, of such Girls as in their Hinder Parts, and their Fore Parts, and in whatsoever Parts did suffer them most, lamentably Cruelly. . . ."[8] Red Cross undoubtedly recalls Spenser's Red Cross Knight in *The Faerie Queen*. Here, however, the Knight's traditional purity is parodied in Evangeline's mission to provide sexual relief for young women.

Introducing the theme of human passion and specifically, lesbian sexuality, the narrator mocks middle-class ideas of moral progress and human superiority. She implies humorously that passion rules human nature: ". . . from the day that we were indifferent Matter, to this wherein we are Imperial Personages of the divine human Race, no thing so solaces it as other Parts as inflamed, or with the Consolation every woman has at her Finger Tips, or at the very Hang of her Tongue?" (p. 6)

Barnes's humor, building on puns, understatement, and circumlocutions, not only attacks middle-class ideas but is used to undermine readers' confidence in various characters. She thus continues the practice, demonstrated in *Ryder* and in various other early works, of introducing a character and then also questioning the values of that character. In *Ladies Almanack* Maisie Tuck-and-Frill and Patience Scalpel challenge Evangeline Musset's earthy creed. For example, Maisie Tuck-and-Frill is presented as one conscious of spiritual realities, yet the spoonerism of her name wittily undermines that seriousness of purpose. Readers are amused but tentative in responding to her character and ideas. Are Maisie's values to be trusted? Or those of Evangeline Musset? Barnes's humor achieves a distancing effect that is reinforced by the deliberate ambiguity of her prose.

Impenetrable, Barnes's prose, cat-like, plays with deliberate contradiction and the reader's understanding. One of the most oblique passages, found in "February," establishes the thematic contest between loving and writing, illuminating as it does so the limitations of earthly love. "February" refines the idea raised by Patience Scalpel in "January": how is one to live? The narrator begins: "This be a Love Letter for a Present . . ." (p. 14). The referent for "This" is unclear, though one may presume that the speaker refers to the book itself. If so, the speaker presents herself as one who would gain the attention of Evangeline Musset. The problem is attracting the attention of one who has many others around her: "Then what shall I for her that hath never been accomplished?" (p. 15). The elliptic prose invites a reader to recognize the "that" clause as adjectival, modifying "her." However, this interpretation produces a clear contradiction, since the reader already knows of Musset's prowess. Thus, the alternative is to read the clause as a noun clause, that is, what thing that has never been done successfully before can I do for her? Implicitly, the answer is to write a book that celebrates Musset's life; the narrator reinforces this idea by enumerating the difficulties of gaining her notice through metaphors which point to writing:

> Shall one stumble on a Nuance that twenty Centuries have not pounced upon, yea worried and made a Kill of? . . . Will she unpack her Panels for such a Stale Receipt, pour out her Treasures for a coin worn thin? . . .
> . . . *To have been the First,* that alone would have gifted me! (Pp. 16–17)

The phrases related to writing, taken together with *"To have been the first,"* refer to the difficulty of writing about love, a topic sufficiently written about already, or, on a sexual level, to the difficulty of winning a love who can be and is won by just about anyone. The language is deceptively double in correlating being "gifted" with receiving inspiration, or with receiving the lover.

An alternative the narrator explores is to renounce the lover or the task of writing and thereby "become a Monument to No-Ability for her sake?" The pun echoes in various ways: "no-ability" may imply lacking skill in writing or loving; or "no-ability," the ability to say "no"; or the opposite "know-ability, namely capable of being "known." In effect, Barnes plays with understanding as penetration. Through the multiple possibilities of the pun, the narrator rejects, apparently, renouncing either writing or her pursuit. Readers can only be certain that "therein is no way for me," implies some kind of rejection of some aspect of the lover, though the narrator continues the ambiguous levels of lover/writer by asserting that "Fancy," that is, the imagination (liking is also a possibility) is the narrator's only "Craft," or ability, or deceit, in the sense of "representing as true what is known to be false." In addition, the narrator later refers to *craft* as wisdom (p. 59). Through her craft, she implies, she has the ability to see the lover as she will, or that imagining the lover is her ability rather than emulating her, or winning her, by action.

The effect of the ambiguity here is to keep two "ways" suspended in a kind of irresolvable tension: loving—perhaps in spite of reservations—and creating. Thus, *Ladies Almanack* promises to be a curiously honest love letter: the narrator may be a lover who chooses to remain apart, and/or the lover, a writer who chooses to celebrate a life that attracts her but that also seems at some level questionable.

The lover/writer ambiguity was a theme that appealed to Barnes, perhaps because she recognized in the autobiographical nature of her fiction the "voyeuristic" attention Barnes-the-writer devoted to Barnes-the-lover. Katya and Moydia of "The Grande Malade," which first appeared in *This Quarter* (1925), enact such relationship: Katya in observing and reporting Moydia's story is the artist, an observor who creates a reality that is superior to life while also reflecting it.[9] Similarly, in *Ladies Almanack*, readers observe the heroine Evangeline Musset—who reflects the straying ways of Natalie Clifford Barney, Barnes's friend, and the infidelity of Thelma Wood, Barnes's lover—and the narrating voice who celebrates but also questions Musset's life. In this regard the book is both tribute and perhaps subtext warning on personal and universal levels.

Barnes's ambiguous prose and the technique of thematic juxtaposition she employs invite readers to search for patterns and connections that may resolve apparent contradictions but to recognize also that the complexity of experience may not be resolved in traditional, or logical, patterns. In *Ladies Almanack* her plot has the thematic consistency of the almanack form that is peculiarly suited to Barnes's predilection for bringing together opposing ideas, a trait evident in her early plays where characters confront one another, often in antagonistic tones, revealing opposing ideas and concepts of life. Gheid Storm and Helena Hucksteppe of "To the Dogs" are typical examples. Storm has been raised by "upright women," and his actions reflect a judgmental attitude toward passion, while Helena has accepted her sensual nature without apology or repression.

Barnes's use of form and allegorical characters in *Ladies Almanack* creates the semblance of a morality play stage. At the center of the stage stands Evangeline Musset, surrounded by those who question her values, bringing together the themes of heterosexual and lesbian love, earthly love, and the desire for transcendence. As lesbian crusader, Evangeline parodies Ryder's self-appointed messianic role by seeking "converts" to her creed. In doing so, she supplants patriarchal principle and the principle of "nature," represented in *Ryder* by Wendell Ryder. In addition, Musset whimsically reflects the soul's search for a satisfactory way of life. In the course of her life she has advocated lesbianism, then the wisdom of indifference, only to discover that wisdom too is vanity. Then she resigns herself calmly to her physical nature—sensual and mortal—and dies peacefully at the age of ninety-nine. Thus, the work seems a celebration of lesbian love—if readers focus primarily on Evangeline Musset's career, which provides the attraction of a modest narrative line.

However, more important is the idea of created order that Musset represents. On one level, as lesbian she is self-creating and self-determined; neither the role she establishes in life nor her sphere of activity is a matter of biological destiny. In this context lesbianism is not only literally a sexual preference, it is also a symbol of consciously ordered life. Evangeline, as lesbian, represents generation by ideas, an imagined reality, as opposed to Ryder's natural generation. In a special sense, then, she is an emblem of the artist, creating a life by imagination.

The garden imagery associated with her reinforces the idea of consciously ordered reality. In the introduction she is associated with Venus; her coterie, in "September," with the Garden of Venus. The garden imagery, reaching back to medieval allegory, suggests a cultivated place, which, as a result of its cultivation, is artificial; therefore, it is also superior to the uncontrolled, unordered natural world. Yet garden imagery, by tradition, is strictly temporal, that is, associated with the present, earthly reality. Thus, even if Musset's reality is an ordered one, the result of human imagination, it is nevertheless limited. Evangeline Musset's world is consciously tuned to the present.

Despite the positive aspect of Musset's acceptance of the fleeting present, her dedication to passion, the worldly and temporal, is opposed by Patience Scalpel, Maisie Tuck-and-Frill, and the narrator—all of whom provide perspectives critical of Evangeline Musset's views.

Death is no surprise to Patience Scalpel. When Evangeline bemoans the inevitable presence of death, represented in Daisy Downpour's courtship of her, Patience merely observes, "Time passes" (p. 68). Patience's awareness, signified by her name, which is sufficiently ambiguous to avoid an easy translation, is one that provides a touchstone of life. "Patience," of course, implies the capacity to endure, or to bear. Though "Scalpel" has suggested "acerbic wit" to various critics, Patience is, we remember from the opening in "January," concerned with the continuity of life; her daughters will marry rather than give themselves to the "passing moment." Therefore, she seems also a reminder of mortality.

Another character who is a foil to Evangeline Musset is Masie Tuck-and-Frill. Maisie also injects a chastening influence on the earthy spirit of Musset. Appearing in "March," Maisie is described as having "a Trade too tender for Oblivion" (p. 22).[10] Her speech is nearly untranslatably epigrammatic: "A Man's love is built to fit Nature. Woman's is a Kiss in the Mirror. It is a Farewell to the Creator, without disturbing him, the supreme Tenderness toward Oblivion . . ." (p. 23).

Musset concludes from this speech that Maisie sounds as if she should be one of them. The passage obliquely opposes male love—nature and generation—with a woman's conscious acceptance of the present only—"a Kiss in the Mirror"—a willingness to accept oblivion without making demands on a future. Maisie, however, confesses that her voice is "the Voice of the Prophet: Those alone who sit in one Condition, their Life through, know what the plans were, and what the Hopes are, and where the Spot the two lie, in that Rot you call your Lives." The description of prophet suggests contemplative aloofness, or, again, the artist—"a Trade too tender for Oblivion."

Like Patience, Maisie alludes to the passage of time, and concludes, "I would that the Mind's Eye had not been so bent upon the Heart" (p. 23). When Evangeline answers that "It's a good Place," Maisie returns, "A good place indeed, but a better when seen Indirectly." Though her meaning remains suspended because of the vagueness of "indirectly," she nevertheless alludes to values other than the concern with love which Evangeline represents. She does not criticize lesbian love per se, but she objects to her singleminded devotion to love.

Thus, Patience Scalpel and Maisie Tuck-and-Frill, having in common some idea of a value that transcends the present, have countered Musset's devotion to love. Patience Scalpel claims not to understand lesbian love; she affirms nature with her interest in her daughters' marrying, but Maisie seems approving, though she stands apart. Her attitude is similar to that of the narrator who has claimed in "February," "therein is no way for me." The effect, so far, of the opposition between Musset and Patience and Maisie has been to broaden the context of the dialogue to include all love—whether lesbian or hetereosexual.

The narrator continues to question the value of love in several scenes, which are directly satirical of lesbian love, but whose effect is to draw parallels between lesbian and heterosexual love. In "March," for example, Lady Buck-and-Balk and Tilly-Tweed-in-Blood come to enlist Evangeline's help in supporting legislation to allow lesbian marriage.

Immorality should no more exist among lesbians than heterosexuals, they argue. They can hardly expect much sympathy from the crusading Musset, who converts as she pleases. No matter, Barnes's point is a satirical observation that everywhere there are those who would legislate for the rest.

In "July" and "August" the narrator casts a satirical look at the language of love, infidelity, and the evil of bragging. These sections, showing the folly of love, continue the linking of loving and writing. In "July" the narrator remarks that "with an unwilling Hand," she reports "what a woman says to a Woman and she be up to her Ears in Love's Acre" (p. 42). The section comments wryly on unfaithfulness:

> I may have trifled in my Day, or in Days to come, or today itself; or even now be rifling Hours for the penning of this to you, but though I gather dear Daffodils abroad, plunge Head first into many a Parsley Field, tamper with high strung and low lying; though I press to my Bosom the very Flower of Women, or tire myself to a prostrate Portion, without a Breath between me and her; toss her over the off-leg to bring her to rights, say never that I do not adore you as my only and my best. (P. 44)

The narrator breaks off, condemning the quality of the prose:

> It is worse than this ! More dripping, more lush, more lavender, more mid-mauve, more honeyed, more Flower-casting, more Cherub-bound, more downpouring, more saccharine, more lamentable, more gruesomely unmindful of Reason or Sense, to say nothing of Humor. . . . (Pp. 45–46)

By pointing out the prose excesses and pairing them comically with the insincere lover, the narrator raises infidelity as an issue. In "August" she attacks gossips and braggarts, comparing heterosexual and lesbian lovers: "just as there are some Fellows who will brag that they can teach a Woman much," there are also women "no wiser, who maintain that they could (had they a Mind to) teach a taught Woman . . ." (p. 50).

The point of these passages is that woman's folly in love is equal to or greater than that of men. If men talk of their affairs, so do women; if men brag of their prowess so, unfortunately, do women. These satirical passages, in detailing flaws within the lesbian society, show the basic effect of passion on the human spirit, whether love is lesbian or heterosexual. The comparisons suggest that if lesbian love is no better than heterosexual love, neither is it any worse. However, the perspective that love is ruinous business gains force through the autumn months.

In "September" the narrator argues that the torture which men and women suffer because of jealousy is futile pride, giving false importance to the present:

> For all are bagged of the same Net, and one comes to as ignoble Ashes as another. The pelvic Bone of Saint Theresa gapes no more Honesty than that of Messalina, for the missing Door wherein no Man passed, is as Not as that windy Space where all were wont to charge, . . .
>   . . . She is dishonest to-day, but tomorrow she is unsought forever. (P. 56)

Far from a celebration of lesbian love, "September," in a tone despairing of human achievement of wisdom, points out the frustration and limitation of all earthly love. The narrator argues for indifference, a stoic detachment, as remedy to the folly of love and jealousy:

> . . . we trouble the Earth awhile with our Fury; our Sorrow is flesh thick, and we shall not cease to eat of it until the easing Bone. Our Peace is not skin deep, but to the Marrow, we are not wise this side of *rigor mortis* ; we go down to no River of Wisdom, but swim alone in Jordan. We have few Philosophers among us, for our Blood was stewed too thick to bear up Wisdom, which is a little Craft, and floats only when the way is prepared, and the Winds are calm. (P. 59)

In "October" the human need for a transcendent value is introduced allegorically. Woman is personified. In her forlorn condition she (Woman) "saw that her Years were mounting, and she returned homeward, and Godless and fearless, made Fear and God of the yellow Hair of Dame Musset . . ." (p. 63). As one aspect of Daisy Downpour's identity is courtship, the other death and a longing for transcendence, Daisy's dual identity opposes the desire for permanence and transcendence to Evangeline's earth-centered and temporal creed. Evangeline sees in Daisy Downpour's veneration Woman's need to affirm importance, or meaning, beyond fleeting impressions, and she objects: "I fear that, in yonder Bosom leaning upon her Casement, grows a Garden of Hope, and that with it she would crown and feather me with the Pinions of celestial Glory only to destroy me with these same Implements . . ." (p. 67).

In "October" when Evangeline Musset is afflicted and discovers Wisdom, she gives in to the desire for values more lasting than love. In "November" Musset goes about with a new creed: "Never want but what you have, never have but that which stays, and let nothing remain. Wisdom is indifference . . ." (p. 78). However, Musset discovers what the narrator has suggested in "September": mortals, given over to the desires of love, are not very interested in wisdom. Ironically, Musset's indifference to love does not deliver her from "Love and Love's Folly" (p. 77). Instead it attracts even more young women: "the only Trouble with it is how extraordinarily it fills the Bed," Musset confesses. For Musset, love is pleasure, "a better drug than drink."[11]

Despite Musset's failure to convert others to cultivate wisdom, readers are probably inclined to applaud her discovery. First, the long philosophical and religious tradition has prepared most readers to respond positively to wisdom as a suitable response to the uncertainties of life and the emotional trials of love. Second, Musset's acceptance of wisdom seems to produce a welcome snythesis of the conflict developed thus far between her worldliness and the criticism of Patience, Maisie, and the narrator. Dramatically, such a synthesis is very satisfying—but deceptive, for Barnes's denouement is a sudden reversal; Musset discovers that wisdom too is vanity: "At sixty," an old woman tells her, "you are ten Years tired of your Knowledge" (p. 79).

One can easily imagine that Barnes proffered then withdrew such a synthesis because it was too easy thematically, too satisfying structurally, and too welcome to most readers. This unexpected end to Musset's adventure with wisdom signals the eventual triumph of her original creed. "December" marks the death of Dame Musset—unrepentant. A variety of themes—mortality, the torments of love, the futility of wisdom, and a desire for something that transcends human experience—have countered Musset's avowal of wisdom, yet her identification with earthly love is affirmed:

> In this cold and chill December, the Month of the Year when the proof of God died, died Saint Musset, proof of Earth, for she had loosened and come uprooted in the Path of Love, where she had so long flourished. Nor yet with any alien Sickness came she to her Death, but as one who had a grave Commission and the ambassador recalled. (P. 80)

The "December" opening raises some interesting questions: what is referred to as "proof of God"? What is the function of the parallel: proof of God and the death of Musset, proof of earth? The final clause, graced with an outrageous pun, poses an equally interesting question: ambassador from where, or from whom? Another problem, to be addressed before returning to these questions, concerns Musset's funeral. The nature of the ceremony—its exaggerated quality, its mixture of sacred and profane—creates an uneasy response in the reader. Does the ceremony itself undermine Musset's values?

The funeral ceremony is salaciously secular, playing off religious tradition in such a way that even Lanser, one of Barnes's most appreciative critics, experiences "discomfort." The troublesome passage portrays, according to Lanser, a "sexual communion" as it comments on the tongue that "would not suffer ash": "The glorification of the tongue as the ultimate sexual instrument must surely have provided an antidote to the ethos of phallic supremacy and clitoral insufficiency of a newly Freudian age."[12]

While Lanser focuses on the "sexual communion" of the funeral passage, I would suggest that "tongues," in addition to the level of sexual innuendo, carries a second meaning, typical of the sexual/spiritual context. A tongue of flame traditionally implies divine inspiration. Thus, Barnes merges three concepts—love, divinity, and sexuality—into one symbol. In doing so, Barnes suggests that love is not only the source of divinity and creativity within human nature, but also the satanic, the limitation of human nature.

The tongue that plays upon the handful that "had been she indeed" is metaphorically the spirit of the artist who transforms the "she indeed" into a richly complex symbol, affirming the diversity and uncertainty of daily life and the transcendent impulse that inspires the work of art. The funeral ceremony, despite its mixture of comic, sexual, and sacred, therefore, does not undermine Musset's values. Her belief in earthly love is not discredited by the reality of the limitations of love; she triumphs in spite of them. Conversely, neither is the narrator discredited as foolish or nagging—the limitations of love and the need to transcend them are also impressively real.

One further reference, which pulls together the secular and sacred echoes inherent in the burial passage and in the book as a whole, is the inscription on Musset's urn, "O ye of little faith." The phrase recalls Christ's response to the disciple Thomas who asked to see Christ's wounds. The biblical passage condemns those who demand proof for their faith, and here may indict those who remain skeptical of Musset's faith that love—earthly love—is an abiding reality. Or, playing upon the "ambassador recalled" suggestion, the phrase "O ye of little faith" connects earthly and spiritual love and implies that those who demand evidence of spiritual realities are bound to be disappointed. On yet another level, the phrase may also indict the followers of Musset, who, in their elaborate ceremony, distort what she represents by enshrining it, as Daisy Downpour has done.

Thus, the phrase "O ye of little faith" addresses various audiences in *Ladies Almanack*, or readers themselves, but it fails to clarify a final position between the two views of life presented: earthly or transcendent values. One trait shared by the potential audiences, including readers, is the desire for certainty, or some resolution of contradictory themes. But Barnes has been very careful to preclude resolution. In fact, creating an experience of uncertainty, a sense that an elusive meaning exists beyond ordinary apprehension, seems one of Barnes's intentions in this work. Accordingly, resolution, or dogmatic certainty, is the last thing a reader should expect. The objective is not to provide a new pattern for the reader, but a new kind of consciousness.

Two points, one in "February," the other in "December," referred to above, reinforce this idea. "December" has begun with an unfinished parallel: "In this cold and chill December, the month of the year when the proof of God died, died Saint Musset, proof of Earth . . ." (p. 80). If Saint Musset is proof of Earth, what is referred to as proof of God? Nature—implying physical nature or a force or principle behind physical nature—is the logical, and traditional, possibility. However, the incomplete term of the parallel may also allude to the rather ambiguous "what we know not," defined by the narrator in "February" as our only "proof of Him." Therefore, the parallel produces: when that sense of mystery dies—what we know not—so dies proof of God; the death implied here is a death of spirit, the death of a readiness, a willingness to engage in uncertainty and possibility, namely life, without forcing its varied appearances into limited certainties. In various ways, Barnes implies that seeking certainty (or proof) or, on another level, self-justification through another (Daisy Downpour's deification of Musset) is failure of spirit.

While *Ladies Almanack* may seem a series of loosely related scenes, the work demonstrates a fine control of characters, mood, and prose—all arranged to examine opposing ideas of love, sexuality, and the role of the artist and imagination. Furthermore, the narrator and Musset function as aspects of a single identity. As lover, Musset is earthly and temporal, devoted to pleasure; as creator, the narrator represents, at least figuratively, Musset's alter ego: the artistic desire for transcendence, the creature who watches the lover and out of that disorder and suffering creates that which transcends that suffering and that life. This difficult relationship between living and suffering and creativity presented in the contrasting claims of the narrator and Evangeline Musset can be resolved only in the work of art itself. Barnes, in giving substance to this idea, demonstrates the belief that the order of the human imagination is superior to ordinary reality, but dependent upon it as well.

In "February" the narrator has suggested that "This be a Present." Therefore, the book is a gift of love, expressing views of the value of love and its limitations in contradictory, and unreconciled, tension. In a special sense, the narrator, as figurative writer, resolves the problem of loving versus creating established in "February": by creating the work of art she affirms earthly love, its limitations, and the desire to transcend both. Only the artificial creation of the artist, the work of art, is able to embrace the contradictions of the daily present, and aspire, by doing so, to the permanent. Indeed, the tongue "that would not suffer ash" of *Ladies Almanack* is the work of art itself.

Conclusion

Reading Barnes has never been easy, yet it continues to be rewarding. As we come to understand the artistry in Barnes's work, her world vision becomes clearer and her stature as an artist grows. In the early work Barnes focused on the individual in conflict with the realities of the external world and with inner demands. This work reflects the decadent awareness that middle-class values, including the desire for success and respectability, represent timid evasions of human mortality. The early journalistic pieces directly criticize middle-class conformity and show that Barnes had little faith in moral progress or in human nature in general.

Beneath Barnes's attack on middle-class conventions is an awareness of the repressive effect they exert on the identity of the individual. For Barnes, as for Gourmont earlier, denial of sexual nature was destructive. Nearly all of Barnes's plays address sexuality, from the witty look at Sheila's hypocrisy in *An Irish Triangle*, to the comic liberation of Amelia and Vera in *The Dove*. Yet from another perspective sexuality can also be destructive of identity. By the time of *Ryder* and *Ladies Almanack* a cautionary note is raised. While middle-class attitudes toward sexuality continue to be satirized, Barnes pointed also the danger of adopting sexual freedom as the liberating principle of human nature. In *Ryder*, in particular, exaggerated sexuality represents a distortion of the human spirit and an evasion of mortality. In *Ladies Almanack* exaggerated sexuality is questioned but eventually incorporated by the artistic spirit— transcended but neither denied nor degraded: it is a reality of the human condition.

But it was not the only reality. Throughout Barnes's work runs the thread of mortality. Sven Ahman's dramatic headline on *The Antiphon*'s première crystallizes the importance of this theme in Barnes's work: "Controversial Genius: Exclusive U.S. Authoress in World Premiere at

Dramatic Theatre: 'I Wrote Because I Was to Die.' " Barnes's handling of this theme included graphic representations of death, as in "The Nigger," collected in *A Night among the Horses,* and the satirical thrusts of Lydia Steptoe who worried that people led "dreary and wasteful lives" rather than "lay themselves open" to charges of a tasteless death by committing an inappropriate suicide. Confronted with mortality, Barnes insisted on the necessity of ordering experience. She asserted the claims of the mind and spirit—without assuming a religious orthodoxy. The artist, that is, the superior sensibility, accepts personal nature, including sexuality and mortality; and imagination shapes and transforms the personal existence into a universal and enduring truth. Death is not to be preferred, for life, tragic as it may often be, is all we have. Barnes's criticism of human nature, in the words of Lydia Steptoe, was that "few men dignify their hazardous mortality with immortal purpose."[1]

Like O'Neill, Eliot, Faulkner, and other practitioners of what some have called the international style, Barnes belongs in the tradition of literary experimentation, heir of symbolist ideas and practices. Yet she is also very much a part of American tradition in reflecting the journey of the soul to conscious moral awareness. Barnes's plays and short fiction show characters who face their nature and those who have evaded that recognition. Many who accept their nature stand outside of society and its values. On the one hand, Helena of *To the Dogs* is alone, but strong in her isolation. On the other hand, Kate of *Three from the Earth* denies her sensual nature, but upholds conventional respectability by marrying a supreme court judge.

In the short fiction social pressures are less important; Barnes emphasizes the consciousness of her characters. Though different in style and manner from Henry James or Edith Wharton, Barnes, like them, considers the drives that motivate her characters in their search for values by which they can live. This search or longing that is at the center of Barnes's work is examined humorously in one of Barnes's *Theatre Guild* sketches. Brother Sumac—whose name is a play on the idea of the fall and also the theological idea of a fortunate fall—questions "the passion in the human heart to be something it is not." He expresses uncertainty whether this ambition is "a true aspiration or a terrible and unholy criticism of the Most High."[2] He adds that though he wants to be good, he has been "fashioned exceedingly evil." Sumac comically balances one perspective against another: Is such an aspiration a fulfillment of divine nature or a criticism of the extent to which we are motivated by physical nature? In implying that if it is one, it is also the other, Barnes demonstrates a cunning irreverence like that of Twain whose characters question the goodness of a god who had also brought so much evil into the world. Posing the question implies the risk of nihilism as an answer, and

Barnes faced this possibility, neither affirming nor denying. Though many of Barnes's characters are defeated, there are also those, like the princess, who achieve a vital equilibrium between inner and outer destructive forces. In Barnes's world such balance is a victory.

Barnes had few illusions about her own nature or human nature in general; nevertheless, she assumed that human potential existed to take hold of life rather than live in evasion. In 1965 she wrote to Peggy Guggenheim, ". . . I believe people only really 'live', [sic] and function, (at least, at their best) when they honour something personified by someone . . [sic] Someone whom you cannot possibly let down."[3] The comment confirms that Barnes saw the individual as capable of moral choice and action, though perhaps not necessarily predisposed to be so.

Though critics have emphasized her dark vision and her privateness, they have done so at the expense of the embattled vitality at the center of work. Her techniques and style reinforce this vitality. Indirect presentation, juxtaposition of scenes and themes, authorial silence, oblique and indeterminate prose, characters who simultaneously invite identifying and prevent readers from identifying with them—all require the consciousness Barnes thought necessary, all require the balance of discerning engagement. Such was the artistry of Djuna Barnes. Insisting that readers take her on her own terms, she offered what Huysmans had referred to as "an interchange of thought between a magic-working author and an ideal reader, a mental collaboration by consent between half a score persons of superior intellect scattered up and down the world, a delectable feast for epicures and appreciable by them."[4]

Notes

Introduction

1. See, for example, Donald J. Greiner's "Djuna Barnes' *Nightwood* and the American Origins of Black Humor," *Critique* 17 (1975): 45–54.

2. J.-K. Huysmans, "Preface" (1903), *Against the Grain*, trans. from *A Rebours* (1884; rpt., New York: Illustrated Editions, 1931), 53, 68.

3. Glenn S. Burne, ed. and trans. *Remy de Gourmont: Selected Writings.* (Ann Arbor: University of Michigan Press, 1966), 179–80.

4. Anna Balakian, *The Symbolist Movement: A Critical Appraisal* (New York: Random House, 1967), 101.

5. Charles Baudelaire, "Le Crépuscule du Matin," trans. David Paul in *Flowers of Evil: A Selection*, eds. Marthiel and Jackson Mathews (New York: New Directions, 1958), 107.

6. Gourmont, *Selected Writings*, 181.

7. Glenn S. Burne, *Remy de Gourmont: His Ideas and Influence in England and America* (Carbondale: University of Southern Illinois Press, 1963), 24.

8. Balakian, 112.

9. Djuna Barnes, "Mordecai Gorelik: A Young Scene Designer Who Seeks, by Using 'Pretense' Rather than 'Illusion,'" to Parade on the Stage the Ceremonial Comedy of the Animal Called Man," *Theatre Guild Magazine* 8 (February 1931): 45.

10. "John Hawkes: An Interview," *Wisconsin Studies in Contemporary Literature* 6 (Summer 1965): 143–44.

Chapter 1. Who Is Lydia?

1. Djuna Barnes to Dan Mahoney, 8 September 1950. This letter and other letters cited are in the Djuna Barnes Papers, McKeldin Library, University of Maryland, College Park.

2. Djuna Barnes to Louis F. Kannenstine, 23 May 1977.

3. Barnes, "Just Getting the Breaks: Donald Ogden Stewart Confides the Secret of World Sucess," *Theatre Guild Magazine* 7 (April 1930): 36.

4. Barnes, "The Washington Square Players: What Is the Secret of the Organization That Started as a Whim in Boni's Bookshop and Now Threatens to Become Popular?" *New York Morning Telegraph, Sunday Magazine*, 3 December 1916, 8.

5. Barnes, "Three Days Out," *New York Morning Telegraph, Sunday Magazine,* 12 August 1917, 4.

6. Barnes, "Giving Advice on Life and Pictures: One Must Bleed His Own Blood," *New York Morning Telegraph, Sunday Magazine,* 25 February 1917, 7.

7. Barnes, "The Hem of Manhattan," *New York Morning Telegraph, Sunday Magazine,* 29 July 1971, 2.

8. Gourmont, "Le Chemin de velours," in *Selected Writings,* 175–76.

9. Barnes, "David Belasco Dreams: The Chronicles of One Who Wanders among the Heavy Timbers of Antiquity," *New York Morning Telegraph, Sunday Magazine,* 31 December 1916, 1.

10. The regularity of the question prompts speculation regarding Barnes's own feelings. Near this time, 1917–18, Barnes married Courtney Lemon, a man later associated with the Theatre Guild, though the marriage appears to have failed by the summer of 1919. Lawrence Lagner refers to the marriage in *The Magic Curtain.*

11. Barnes, "Giving Advice on Life and Pictures," 7.

12. Barnes, "Becoming Intimate with the Bohemians: When the Dusk of a Musty Hall Has Crept through the Ever Widening Keyhole the Queen of Bohemia Has Arisen, for Her Day Has Begun; You Will Find Her in Polly's, the Candle Stick, the Brevoort, the Black Cat or Any Other Greenwich Village Place You Care to Visit," *New York Morning Telegraph, Sunday Magazine,* 19 November 1916, 4.

13. G. B., "Fleurs Du Mal a la Mode de New York,"*Pearson's Magazine,* 45 (December 1919): 656.

14. Barnes, "The Songs of Synge: The Man Who Shaped His Life as He Shaped His Plays," *New York Morning Telegraph, Sunday Magazine,* 18 February 1917, 8.

15. Barnes, "Why Actors?: Brother Sumac Searches for an Answer," *Theatre Guild Magazine* 7 (December 1929): 43.

16. Barnes, "Wilson Mizner—of Forty-Fourth Street: The Address Is Important for He Says He Has Not Been North, South, East, or West of It in as Many Years," *New York Morning Telegraph, Sunday Magazine,* 24 December 1916, 1.

17. "In Our Village," *Bruno's Weekly* 1 (21 October 1915): 142.

18. Barnes's first book, actually a chapbook, *The Book of Repulsive Women,* was a collection of five drawings and eight "rhythms." It was published by Guido Bruno in November 1915.

19. Harry Burton to Djuna Barnes, 2 November 1925, Djuna Barnes Papers.

20. These articles appeared in *Charm,* January 1925 (pp. 24–25, 95) and March 1925 (pp. 20–21, 94).

21. *Greenwich Villager,* 11 March 1922, n.p.

22. [Lydia Steptoe], "Against Nature: In Which Everything that Is Young, Inadequate and Tiresome Is Included in the Term Natural," *Vanity Fair* 18 (August 1922): 60.

23. [Lydia Steptoe], "Diary of a Dangerous Child: Which Should Be of Interest to All Those Who Want to Know How Women Get the Way They Are," *Vanity Fair* 18 (July 1922): 94.

24. [Steptoe], "What Is Good Form in Dying? In Which a Dozen Dainty Deaths Are Suggested for Daring Damsels," *Vanity Fair* 20 (June 1923): 73.

25. [Steptoe], "Ten-Minute Plays VI: The Beauty," *Shadowland* 9 (October 1923): 43.

26. [Steptoe], "Little Drops of Rain: Wherein Is Discussed the Advantage of XIXth Century Storm over XXth Century Sunshine," *Vanity Fair* 19 (September 1922): 50.

27. Barnes, "Playgoer's Almanack," *Theatre Guild Magazine* 8 (February 1931): 34.

28. Barnes, "Why Actors? Brother Sumac Searches for an Answer," *Theatre Guild Magazine* 7 (December 1929), 42–43.

29. Barnes, "The Dear Dead Days: Love Is Done Differently on Our Current Stage," *Theatre Guild Magazine* 6 (February 1929): 43.

30. Barnes, "Mordecai Gorelik," 45.

31. Barnes, "The Tireless Rachel Crothers: That Vivacious Comedy, *As Husbands Go*, Is the Twenty-fourth which She Has Written in Her Long and Methodical Career," *Theatre Guild Magazine* 8 (May 1931): 17.

32. [Steptoe], "Hamlet's Custard Pie: Giles, the Butler, Learns What Is Wrong with the Drama," *Theatre Guild Magazine* 7 (July 1930): 34–35.

33. Barnes, "'I've Always Suffered from Sirens': Raymond Sovey, however, Has Disciplined His Inspiration so Effectively that He Merges His Stage Settings Completely in the Author's Intention and the Play's Mood," *Theatre Guild Magazine* 8 (March 1931): 23.

34. Barnes, "Mordecai Gorelik," 43–44.

35. Barnes, "Just Getting the Breaks," 35.

36. Barnes must have felt she had succeeded when *Ryder* briefly made the best-seller list, but the type had been struck and by the time it had been reset and the book reissued, public demand had disappeared.

Chapter 2. On the Road to Provincetown

1. Lawrence Langner, *The Magic Curtain* (New York: E. P. Dutton, 1951), 110.

2. Barnes, "Mordecai Gorelik," 43–44.

3. Barnes, "Songs of Synge," 8.

4. "In Our Village," *Bruno's Weekly* 1 (21 October 1915): 142.

5. Barnes, "Death of Life," *New York Morning Telegraph, Sunday Magazine,* 17 December 1916, 8.

6. Barnes, "At the Root of the Stars," *New York Morning Telegraph, Sunday Magazine,* 11 February 1917, 8.

7. The quote is taken from Douglas Messerli's annotations, *Djuna Barnes: A Bibliography* (n.p.: David Lewis, 1975), p. 121. The original review appeared in the *New York Times*, 4 April 1920, sect. 6, p. 6.

8. Barnes, *Kurzy of the Sea*, typescript, p. 3, Djuna Barnes Papers, University of Maryland, College Park. Subsequent page references are indicated in the text.

9. The review is cited in Messerli, p. 120. The review originally appeared in the *Tribune* on 12 January 1920, 12.

10. Barnes, *An Irish Triangle, Playboy* 7 (May 1921): 5.

11. Barnes, *Passion Play, Others* (February 1918): 7, 11.

12. Louis F. Kannenstine, *The Art of Djuna Barnes: Duality and Damnation* (New York: New York University Press, 1977), 135.

13. Barnes, *To the Dogs*, in *A Book* (1923); rpt. in *A Night among the Horses* (New York: Horace Liveright, 1929), 47. The edition used for the second group of plays is *A Night among the Horses*. In the original publication this collection of stories was listed as *A Night Among the Horses*. However, the *Selected Works* edition carries the title, *A Night among the Horses*. Since Barnes revised stories for this collection, it is presumed that this change reflects her wishes. This form is used throughout. Subsequent citations are noted in the text.

14. Jolande Jacobi, *The Way of Individuation* (New York: Harcourt, Brace & World, 1965), 38.

15. Drucker's and Woolcott's reviews are quoted in part in Messerli's *Djuna Barnes,* 119–20. The reviews cited originally appeared in the following newspapers: New York *Tribune,* 16 November 1919, part 4, p. 7; *New York Times,* 9 November 1919, sect. 8.

16. James B. Scott, *Djuna Barnes* (Boston: Twayne Publishing, 1976), 53.

17. Kannenstine, 131.

18. Andrew Field, *Djuna: The Life and Times of Djuna Barnes* (New York: G. P. Putnam's Sons, 1983), 89.

19. Barnes, *Three from the Earth*, in *A Book* (1923); rpt. in *A Night among the Horses*, 18. Subsequent citations are noted in the text.

20. The reviews quoted are cited in Messerli, 121. Originally they appeared in the following newspapers: *New York Times*, 7 May 1926, 12; *New York Evening Post*, 7 May 1926, 14.

21. Barnes, *The Dove* in *A Book* (1923); rpt., *A Night among the Horses* (1929), 149. Subsequent citations are noted in the text.

22. Scott, 59.

23. J. E. Cirlot, *A Dictionary of Symbols*, trans. Jack Sage (New York: Philosophical Library, 1962), 27.

24. Scott, 59.

Chapter 3. Necessary Silence

1. Messerli, 114. The original reviews appeared in the Nashville *Tennessean*, 29 April 1962, sect. D, 10, and in the Washington *Post*, 6 May 1962, sect. E, 6.

2. Suzanne Ferguson, "Djuna Barnes's Short Stories: An Estrangement of the Heart," *Southern Review* 5 (January 1969): 27.

3. Kannenstine, 68, 71.

4. Scott, 24.

5. Ferguson, 41.

6. Barnes, "Jest of Jests," *Smoke and Other Stories*, ed. Douglas Messerli (College Park, Md.: Sun & Moon Press, 1982), 74.

7. "The Coward," *Smoke*, 145. Subsequent citations from *Smoke* are noted in the text.

8. Barnes, "James Joyce; A Portrait of the Man Who is, at Present, One of the More Significant Figures in Literature," *Vanity Fair* 18 (April 1922): 65.

9. Horst Ruthrof, *The Reader's Construction of Narrative* (London: Routledge & Kegan Paul, 1981), 103.

10. Barnes, "The Tireless Rachel Crothers," 18.

11. Messerli, *Smoke*, 19.

12. Kenneth Burke, "Immersion," *The Dial* 76 (May 1924): 461.

13. Barnes, *Selected Works of Djuna Barnes* (New York: Farrar, Straus and Cudahy, 1962), 29. All subsequent references to the collected short stories are from this edition unless noted.

14. *A Night among the Horses*, 196. The quotation appears only in early editions of "The Rabbit," collected in *A Book* and *A Night among the Horses*.

15. Kannenstine, 74.

16. Balakian, 138–39.

17. Scott, 49.

18. Ibid., 30.

19. Ferguson, 34.

20. Kannenstine, 68.

21. Scott, 31.

22. Ferguson, 34.

23. The association may be related to Gourmont's *The Natural Philosophy*. Barnes knew Gourmont's work, and had alluded to him in *Three from the Earth*, though the extent of her knowledge of *The Natural Philosophy* is speculative.

24. Rémy de Gourmont, *The Natural Philosophy of Love*, trans. and postscript by Ezra Pound (New York: Liveright, 1922), 298.

25. Scott, 35.

26. Kannenstine, 72.

27. Ferguson, 40.

28. Barnes, "The Last Petit Souper; (Greenwich Village in the Air—Ahem!)," *Bruno's Weekly* 2, no. 18 (29 April 1916): 667-68, 670.

29. Wallace Fowlie, *Love and Literature: Studies in Symbolic Expression* (Bloomington: Indiana University Press, 1948), 85.

Chapter 4. The Vanity of Ryder's Race

1. Calhoun, L., "A Woman's Hero," *The Arqonaut* 104 (1 September 1928): 12. The *American Mercury* view is quoted in Messerli, 96.

2. These quotations appeared in Messerli, 97–100. The original reviews appeared in the following newspapers: *Toledo* (Ohio) *Times Magazine*, 21 October 1928, 12; New York *Sun*, 18 August 1928, 21; *New Republic* 55 (24 October 1928): 281–83.

3. Field, 31.

4. Scott, 63, 76.

5. Barnes, *Ryder* (New York: Boni & Liveright, 1928; rpt., New York: St. Martin's Press, 1979), 167. All further references are to the reprinted edition.

6. Northrop Frye, *Anatomy of Criticism: Four Essays* (Princeton: Princeton University Press, 1957; rpt. 1973), 309.

7. The source is Samuel Daniel's "Epistle to the Countess of Cumberland," stanza 12.

8. Burne, 24.

9. Morris W. Croll, *"Attic" & Baroque Style: Essays by Morris W. Croll*, ed. J. Max Patrick and Robert O. Evans, with John M. Wallace (Princeton: Princeton University Press, 1966; rpt. 1969), 213.

10. Elizabeth Chappel to Djuna Barnes, 9 May 192(4)? There is general critical agreement that Wendell Ryder is based on Barnes's father. Thus it is interesting that Barnes's mother, Elizabeth Chappell, writes to Djuna in London suggesting that Djuna have Aunt Sue show her the wall where she met Djuna's father. According to her letter, he wore pants patched with green cloth and had white rats about him.

11. Cirlot, 185–86, 259–60. The following summary is taken from Cirlot's commentary.

12. André Gide, "The Reflexive Image," *Journals 1889–1913*, 11 January 1892, excerpted in *The Modern Tradition*, ed. Richard Ellmann and Charles Feidelson, Jr. (New York: Oxford University Press, 1965), 189.

Chapter 5. "A Trade too tender for Oblivion": Ryder's Daugher, Evangeline Musset

1. In an introduction to a 1922 translation of Rémy de Gourmont's *Natural Philosophy of Love*, Burton Rascoe pointed out Gourmont's attack on Christian sexual ideas. In "Dissociation of Ideas," Gourmont had enunciated the pleasure principle in sexual conduct. Similarly, he had defended homosexuality on the grounds that "for certain natures" it is "natural and the only way to happiness . . ." (xix). Gourmont's work and the anonymous publication of *Corydon* (1929) by Gide, arguing for the naturalness of homosexuality, show that traditional sexual morality was hostile to such ideas.

2. Bernard Capp, *Astrology and the Popular Press, English Almanacks, 1500–1800,* (London: Faber & Faber, 1979), 273.

3. Gide's *Corydon* (published anonymously) had defended the naturalness of homosexuality and Radclyffe Hall's *Well of Loneliness* had raised the issue of lesbianism publicly, as had the scandal of Oscar Wilde.

4. Scott, 140.

5. Kannenstine, 53.

6. Field, pp. 126, 127.

7. Susan Sniader Lanser, "Speaking in Tongues: *Ladies Almanack* and the Language of Celebration," *Frontiers* 4 (Fall 1979): 40–41.

8. Djuna Barnes, *Ladies Almanack* (Dijon: Darantiere, 1928; rpt. New York: Harper & Row, 1972), 6. Barnes uses punctuation atypically throughout the text, leaving spaces between the end of the sentence and the appropriate punctuation mark. Her practice has been followed in quoting from the text without further indication of its anamolous nature. Subsequent references are noted in the text.

9. The same theme is fundamental to "The Valet."

10. Maisie's loss of a job parallels Barnes's experience. Barnes went to Paris for Burton Rascoe of *McCall's* in 1922. However, by 1923 she was without a job.

11. Natalie Clifford Barney to Djuna Barnes, Easter 1968, Djuna Barnes Papers.

12. Lanser, 44.

Conclusion

1. [Steptoe], "Hamlet's Custard Pie," 35.

2. Barnes, "Why Actors?" 42–43.

3. Barnes, Letter to Peggy Guggenheim, 22 October 1961.

4. Huysmans, 312.

Works Cited

Primary Sources

Books

A Book. New York: Boni and Liveright, 1923.

Ryder. New York: Boni & Liveright, 1928. Reprint. New York: St. Martin's Press, 1979.

Ladies Almanack. Dijon: Darantiere, 1928. Reprint. New York: Harper & Row, 1972.

A Night Among the Horses. New York: Horace Liveright, 1929.

The Selected Works of Djuna Barnes. New York: Farrar, Straus and Cudahy, 1962.

Smoke and Other Stories. Edited by Douglas Messerli. College Park, Md.: Sun & Moon Press, 1982.

One-Acts

"The Death of Life; 'Death Is the Poor Man's Purse'—Baudelaire." *New York Morning Telegraph, Sunday Magazine* (17 December 1916).

"At the Root of the Stars; A Play in One Act." *New York Morning Telegraph, Sunday Magazine* (11 February 1918).

Passion Play. Others (February 1918), 5–17.

Kurzy of the Sea. (produced 1920) This item is listed under manuscripts.

An Irish Triangle. Playboy 7 (May 1921): 3–5.

Journalism

"The Last Petit Souper." *Bruno's Weekly* (29 August 1916), 665–70.

"Becoming Intimate with the Bohemians; When the Dusk of a Musty Hall Has Crept through the Ever Widening Keyhole the Queen of Bohemia Has Arisen, for Her Day Has Begun; You Will Find Her in Polly's, the Candle Stick, the

Brevoort, the Black Cat or Any Other Greenwich Village Place You Care to Visit." *New York Morning Telegraph, Sunday Magazine* (19 November 1916).

"The Washington Square Players; What Is the Secret of the Organization That Started as a Whim in Boni's Bookshop and Now Threatens to Become Popular?" *New York Morning Telegraph Sunday Magazine* (3 December 1916).

"Wilson Mizner—of Forty-Fourth Street; The Address Is Important for He Says He Has Not Been North, South, East, or West of It in as Many Years." *New York Morning Telegraph, Sunday Magazine* (24 December 1916).

"David Belasco Dreams; The Chronicles of One Who Wanders among the Heavy Timbers of Antiquity." *New York Morning Telegraph, Sunday Magazine* (31 December 1916).

"The Songs of Synge; The Man Who Shaped His Life as He Shaped His Plays." *New York Morning Telegraph, Sunday Magazine* (18 February 1917).

"Giving Advice on Life and Pictures; One Must Bleed His Own Blood." *New York Morning Telegraph, Sunday Magazine* (25 February 1917).

"The Hem of Manhattan." *New York Morning Telegraph, Sunday Magazine* (29 July 1917).

"Three Days Out." *New York Morning Telegraph Sunday Magazine* (12 August 1917).

"James Joyce; A Portrait of the Man Who Is, at Present, One of the More Significant Figures in Literature." *Vanity Fair* 18 (April 1922): 65, 104.

[Steptoe, Lydia]. "Diary of a Dangerous Child; Which Should Be of Interest to All Those Who Want to Know How Women Get the Way They Are." *Vanity Fair* 18 (July 1922): 56, 94.

[Steptoe, Lydia] "Against Nature; In Which Everything that Is Young, Inadequate and Tiresome Is Included in the Term Natural." *Vanity Fair* 18 (August 1922): 60, 88.

[Steptoe, Lydia]. "Little Drops of Rain; Wherein Is Discussed the Advantage of XIXth Century Storm over XXth Century Sunshine." *Vanity Fair* 19 (September 1922): 50, 94.

[Steptoe, Lydia]. "What Is Good Form in Dying? In Which a Dozen Dainty Deaths Are Suggested for Daring Damsels." *Vanity Fair* 20 (June 1923): 73, 102.

[Steptoe, Lydia] "Ten-Minute Plays II: Two Ladies Take Tea." *Shadowland* 8 (October 1923).

[Steptoe, Lydia]. Ten-Minute Plays VI: "The Beauty." *Shadowland* 9 (October 1923): 43, 74.

"The Models Have Come to Town; No Longer Merely the Monopoly of the Artist They Are the Inspiration of Musicians as Well." *Charm* 2 (November 1924): 16, 86, 92.

[Steptoe, Lydia]. "A French General of Fashion; Madame Jenny Sums Up the Secret of Taste: Simple Line, Excellent Texture, Skillful Cut." *Charm* 2 (January 1925): 24–25, 95.

[Steptoe, Lydia] "A French Couturiere to Youth; Dignity, that Is the Thing to Remember After One Is Thirty, Says Madame Jeanne Lanvin." *Charm* 3 (March 1925): 20–21, 71, 94.

[Steptoe, Lydia] "Rome and the Little Theater; Three Directors—Pirandello,

Bragaglia and Ferrari—Have Created an Interest in This Art." *Charm* 6 (August 1926): 15–17, 83.

"The Dear Dead Days; Love Is Done Differently on Our Current Stage." *Theatre Guild Magazine* 6 (February 1929): 41–43.

"Why Actors?; Brother Sumac Searches for an Answer." *Theatre Guild Magazine* 7 (December 1929): 42–43.

"Playgoer's Almanack." *Theatre Guild Magazine* 8 (December 1930): 34–35.

"Just Getting the Breaks; Donald Ogden Stewart Confides the Secret of World Success." *Theatre Guild Magazine* 7 (April 1930), 35–36, 57.

[Steptoe, Lydia]. "Hamlet's Custard Pie: Giles, the Butler, Learns What Is Wrong with the Drama." *Theatre Guild Magazine* 7 (July 1930): 34–35, 48.

"Mordecai Gorelik; A Young Scene Designer Who Seeks, by Using 'Pretense' Rather than 'Illusion,' to Parade on the Stage the Ceremonial Comedy of the Animal Called Man." *Theatre Guild Magazine* 8 (February 1931): 42–45.

"Playgoer's Almanack." *Theatre Guild Magazine* 8 (February 1931): 34–35.

" 'I've Always Suffered from Sirens'; Raymond Sovey, however, Has Disciplined His Inspiration so Effectively that He Merges His Stage Settings Completely in the Author's Intention and the Play's Mood." *Theatre Guild Magazine* 8 (March 1931): 23–25.

"The Tireless Rachael Crothers; That Vivacious Comedy, *As Husbands Go*, Is the Twenty-fourth which She Has Written in Her Long and Methodical Career," *Theatre Guild Magazine* 8 (May 1931), 17–18.

Manuscripts: The Djuna Barnes Papers, McKeldin Library, University of Maryland, College Park

Kurzy of the Sea. [Produced 1920.]

Letter to Natalie Clifford Barney (Easter 1968).

Letter to Peggy Guggenheim (22 October 1961).

Letter to Louis F. Kannenstine (23 May 1977).

Letter to Dan Mahoney (8 September 1950).

Burton, Harry. Letter to Djuna Barnes (2 November 1925).

Chappell, Elizabeth. Letter to Djuna Barnes (9 May 192(4)).

Secondary Sources

Balakian, Anna. *The Symbolist Movement: A Critical Reappraisal.* New York: Random House, 1967.

Baudelaire, Charles. *Flowers of Evil: A Selection.* Edited by Marthiel and Jackson Mathews. New York: New Directions, 1958.

[Bruno, Guido] G. B. "Fleurs Du Mal a la Mode de New York." *Pearson's Magazine* 45 (December 1919).

Burke, Kenneth. "Immersion," *The Dial* 76 (May 1924): 461.

Burne, Glenn S. *Remy de Gourmont: His Ideas and Influence in England and America.* Carbondale: University of Southern Illinois Press, 1963.

Calhoun, L. "A Woman's Hero." *The Argonaut* 104 (1 September 1928): 12.

Capp, Bernard. *Astrology and the Popular Press, English Almanacks, 1500–1800.* London: Faber & Faber, 1979.

Cirlot, J. E. *A Dictionary of Symbols.* Translated by Jack Sage. New York: Philosophical Library, 1962.

Croll, Morris W. *"Attic" & Baroque Style: Essays by Morris W. Croll.* Edited by J. Max Patrick and Robert O. Evans, with John M. Wallace. Princeton: Princeton University Press, 1966. Reprint. 1969.

Ferguson, Suzanne. "Djuna Barnes's Short Stories: An Estrangement of the Heart." *Southern Review* 5 (January 1969): 26–41.

Field, Andrew. *Djuna: The Life and Times of Djuna Barnes.* New York: G. P. Putnam's Sons, 1983.

Fowlie, Wallace. *Love and Literature: Studies in Symbolic Expression.* Bloomington: Indiana University Press, 1948.

Frye, Northrop. *Anatomy of Criticism: Four Essays.* Princeton: Princeton University Press, 1957. Reprint. 1973.

Gide, André. "The Reflexive Image," *The Journals of André Gide, 1889–1913.* In *The Modern Tradition.* Edited by Richard Ellman and Charles Feidelson, Jr. New York: Oxford University Press, 1965.

Gourmont, Rémy de. *The Natural Philosophy of Love.* Translated by Ezra Pound. New York: Liveright, 1922.

––––––. *Remy de Gourmont: Selected Writings.* Edited and translated by Glenn S. Burne. Ann Arbor: University of Michigan Press, 1966.

Greiner, Donald J. "Djuna Barnes' *Nightwood* and the American Origins of Black Humor," *Critique* 17 (1975): 45–54.

Huysmans, J.-K. *Against the Grain.* 1884. Reprint. New York: Illustrated Editions, 1931.

"In Our Village." *Bruno's Weekly* 1 (21 October 1915): 142–43.

Jacobi, Jolande. *The Way of Individuation.* New York: Harcourt, Brace & World, 1965.

"John Hawkes: An Interview," *Wisconsin Studies in Contemporary Literature* 6 (Summer 1965): 140–54.

Kannenstine, Louis F. *The Art of Djuna Barnes: Duality and Damnation.* New York: New York University Press, 1977.

Langner, Lawrence. *The Magic Curtain.* New York: E. P. Dutton, 1951.

Lanser, Susan Sniader. "Speaking in Tongues: *Ladies Almanack* and the Language of Celebration." *Frontiers* 4 (Fall 1979): 39–46.

Messerli, Douglas. *Djuna Barnes: A Bibliography.* N.p.: David Lewis, 1975.

Ruthrof, Horst. *The Reader's Construction of Narrative.* London: Routledge & Kegan Paul, 1981.

Scott, James B. *Djuna Barnes.* Boston: Twayne Publishers, 1976.

W. W. "Home Notes from Abroad: An Interview with Djuna Barnes." *Greenwich Villager* (11 March 1922).

Index